THE COTSWOLD BOY

*From The Coronation
To 'A Hard Day's Night':
A Childhood
In The 50s And 60s*

MARTIN WHITE

APS BOOKS
YORKSHIRE

APS Books
The Stables,
Field Lane,
Aberford
West Yorkshire,
LE25 3AE
www.andrewsparke.com

APS Books is a subsidiary of the APS Publications imprint

THE COTSWOLD BOY

PREFACE

When Laurie Lee's "Cider With Rosie" was published in 1959, my father bought two copies: one for himself and one for his eldest sister. It was an important literary work by one of Britain's leading poets, but also for both of them (born and brought up in the Stroud Valleys in the early 20th Century) a description of locations and even characters whom they actually recalled. Their nostalgia for a world which had slipped away, or at least altered much, was almost palpable as they discussed the book in our family home! Into relief were thrown the dramatic changes due to the Depression and World War II, but also the more subtle, insidious, yet far-reaching erosion of a way of life due to the arrival of the motor car and other technological advances, such as the refrigerator and what my parents regarded at first as a social evil: the tv.

Sixty-three years on, perspective has again shifted. The worlds of the Lee family in Slad and of my own around 1960 at Rodborough, only a few miles distant, appear to have had so much more in common than my father and aunt would ever have credited, and both periods now seem rather alien.

This memoir is no "Cider With Rosie". It is instead a simple attempt to portray life for a young child in that alien world, which was post-War, but pre-Permissive Society; where old attitudes and superstitions persisted, and where (certainly among older folk) there was still a strong local dialect rooted in the language of the Saxons:

"th' bist" – modern English "you are"[1],
"th' bis'n't" / "the bis'n a" (before a verb) – modern English "you are not"[2].

Culturally, the Stroud Valleys still do have a distinct personality, not belonging to the Cotswold plateau or the Severn Valley, but it is one that has evolved a long way from that of the 1960s, let alone the 1920s, and the dialect has waned.

In each period, the geography has, of course, played a role. Five valleys radiate out from Stroud itself: those of Chalford, Nailsworth, Slad, Painswick and Ruscombe, and all are enclosed by fairly high Cotswold

---

[1] Modern German „du bist".
[2] Modern German "du bist nicht".

Hills, except to the West where the valley around Stonehouse broadens out to merge with that of the Severn itself. There must always have been a tendency for the area to turn in on itself and become its own little world: more difficult to sustain in the globally-aware digitised 2020s; much easier in my youth, when a trip to Gloucester was a major event, when we as a family usually went away for an annual holiday, but few of the people we knew ever went abroad.

If I felt central to that world, it was of course the delusion of childhood that everything revolves around oneself, but that fancy was fed by the fact we lived near the top of Rodborough Hill, which dominates the town and both the Chalford and Nailsworth Valleys, and from which the other three valleys can be seen in the distance. That old delusion maybe persists in persuading me that I may now dare take on the role of portraying the area at that time.

In my eighth decade, though, I have other excuses, not least the desire to record those whom I loved and their way of behaving and speaking, and their earthy sense of humour. For soon none will be left who recall them at all. My relatives (now almost all dead) and a few friends who have remained dear to me are named in the text. Ironically, due to the current culture and law relating to privacy, the many other individuals whom I well recall and to whom I refer are for the most part cloaked in aliases, since I have no way of contacting them and securing their approval of my words. This is true of most of the children with whom I was at school, though I trust that in no way this undermines the picture of education itself in the late 50s and early 60s, which it has been one of my main objectives to describe.

Education in fact provides the climax of this memoir – in so far as a memoir can ever have a climax. My family's move from Rodborough to Gloucester in 1963 highlighted the considerable differences between schooling in the Stroud Valleys and that in the nearby city. Adjusting from one to the other was for me quite a painful experience, though one from which my life has benefitted ever since. In retrospect, education and my experience of it encapsulated how much nearer Stroud in the 60s was to Stroud in the 20s, whereas Gloucester had at least a more modern feel.

Martin White

CHAPTER 1

Just below the Common on the left as you descend Rodborough Hill is a row of eighteenth-century stone cottages. They are not built parallel to the road, nor do they match its downward slope, but veer off at an angle towards the south-west, all more or less at the same elevation. They occupy a small spur, with commanding views over the Nailsworth and Chalford Valleys, and over Stroud itself. It was here that I spent most of the first ten years of my life between 1955 and 1963.

Four of the cottages (Nos 1-4 Rock Cottages) form a terrace, and then a fifth (Rock View) is detached and set much further back. My family, the Whites, lived at No 4, which was at the end of the terrace. Where the rear of our house overlapped with the front portion of "Rock View" there was a narrow passageway, open to the sky. Every south-west gale would funnel from the Severn Estuary, up along the narrowing Stroud Valleys, until it reached maximum force passing through that passage – or so it seemed!

No 1 Rock Cottages fronted directly on to the road with its own gate, had its own garden at the back, and was walled off from the rest of the terrace. Ernie Cook and his wife lived there, and because they were so "walled off" and self-contained, we had little to do with them. The other properties, however, shared a common access, and so to a greater or less extent their occupants shared in each others' lives. The actual access from the street was by means of a stone step up from the pavement and through a gap in iron railings. A broad pathway then ran in front of Nos 2 and 3 over compacted gravel to a black metal gate set between two low grey brick walls, which led to our own house. My parents were always keen this gate should be kept closed, especially after my sister was born.

"Please close the gate. Toddler on the loose," my father inscribed on a small hardboard sign, which he attached once she was mobile.

The pathway then skirted the front of our house, passing our two small and sunless "lawns" on the right, then turned left between my mother's beds of wallflowers, before arriving at Rock View, which had in front of it a large paved area with a large metal flower pot in its middle. (This concealed the shaft of an old well.) Rock View, which was owned by the Heaven family, was in many ways the most desirable of the residences: it was detached; it was furthest from the road – an advantage in a time when none of the families had a car to park; it had that rather attractive paved area; and in front of that, only a few yards from the house itself, was its sizeable vegetable patch.

By comparison, the arrangement of garden land for the other cottages was bizarre. The old lady at No 2 (Margey Bates) was fortunate. She had a garden which ran along the backs of her cottage, No 3 (owned by the Gardiners) and No 4. It was separated from each of those houses by a meandering paved pathway.

Nos 3 and 4 were, however, much less fortunate, being entirely divorced from their own gardens. If you had been able to fly over the line of cottages, you would have seen those gardens, not in any way adjacent to their respective cottages, but on the far side of Rock View. Access to them added another level of complication. Whereas the most direct route would have been across the paved area in front of Rock View, **that** was Mrs Heaven's exclusive paved area, and, for the adults at least, it was wise to respect Mrs Heaven's property rights! Instead, we (the Whites) had to follow a narrow buddleia-bedecked pathway which passed down the far side of Heavens' garden between it and the back of the top storey of another house which was itself constructed further down the hill! This belonged to a Scottish lady known as "Mrs Mack", though whether her name really was "Mrs Mack", or whether it was "Mrs Mac-something else" it never occurred to me to ask.

The owners of Rock View, Stella and Tom Heaven, were in late middle age. Tom still worked at a factory, but seemed to spend the rest of his time at home - in Summer either tending the garden, or sitting outside his back door, reading the paper, or simply ruminating. Sometimes he would impart to us the gist of his thoughts, which could be along the lines of: "An't there been a lotta changes since I were a boy?" or "I d' sit 'ere watchin' the sun. 'Ee d' rise over there and 'ee d' set over there."

He told my parents on several occasions that as a young man he had gone by bus to Cirencester, but hadn't known anyone, so he'd come straight back! His wife, Stella, was more adventurous. She would at least go to Gloucester or maybe even Cheltenham on a shopping expedition, but, that said, neither of them ever took a holiday.

Stella and Tom had had four children: three daughters and then a son. The eldest was already married and had a daughter. Another daughter married and moved away whilst we lived next door, and their one son, who played a trumpet – very loudly – made a career with Woolworths and went to l live in East Anglia as soon as he could. The Heavens had not yet, however, managed to divest themselves of the rest of their family. Their middle daughter, Jean, had moved away, but had been widowed as the result of a motor-bike accident, and had had to return to her parents' home with her two small children, Roger (fair and gangling) and Brenda (dark haired and dimpled). This arrangement subsisted for the full eight and a half years we were their neighbours, and for several years afterwards, and Roger and Brenda became my main friends and playmates.

Whilst, as an infant, I was oblivious to any such under-currents, it was clear to my parents that the presence of Roger and Brenda in the household was something which sometimes caused friction with Tom and Stella. This made it the more embarrassing that Stella rather took to me and seemed to think that I, or at least the things I came out with, were wonderful. I would go round and lecture her on whatever was interesting me at the time, and she would indulge me and report back to my mother later. She handled it well when one day in 1959, when I was six, I went round and demanded to know if she had voted for Mr MacMillan (as my parents had done).

"Not this time, Martin. Not this time!" she said. Despite my nascent political fervour, I accepted this with good grace.

The Gardiners at No 3 – Edie and Ernie – were a more elderly couple. They had no children of their own, and once my sister was old enough to totter round to their cottage, they came to dote on her. She christened them "Gargher" to start with, but that evolved into "the Gardies": a name we all used after a while. They were a strange contrast: she had a pale complexion and always wore a hairnet, could be rather stern, had strong opinions, and went to church; he was far more relaxed and fun-loving, eyes twinkling with amusement in a sun-bronzed face. They would argue with each other, but she always won with a definitive: "You be wrong, Ern!"

As my sister became more and more the darling of No 3, and perhaps in reaction, I traded on my entrée at Rock View and was encouraged to do so by Stella. Yet even without this unspoken competition for our childish affections, there seemed always to have been a certain antipathy between the Heavens and the Gardies, which was rooted in the past - way beyond our ken and not to be enquired into – but exacerbated by the Gardiners' habit of short-cutting across Mrs Heaven's frontage and not using the buddleia-bedecked pathway behind Mrs Mack's! Sensitive to this situation, my parents performed a balancing act, keeping on good terms with both families throughout the time we were, by reason of geography, the buffer between them. My parents were friendly, but respectful to both, always calling them "Mr and Mrs Gardiner" and "Mr and Mrs Heaven", at least to their faces, whilst the neighbours themselves (with the advantage of years) used my parents' Christian names (Jack and Phyl.) Edie signed my sister's baby card "E and E Gardiner", as became her status.

The final resident of the terrace (at No 2) was Margey Bates: a very old lady, if not a witch. She wore thick black skirts right down to the ground, with a white embroidered bodice above. She walked with crutches, since she had a withered leg, which may have dictated the length of her skirts, though they were also simply the clothes she had been wearing since the Victorian era. We rarely spoke to Margey, because she kept herself to herself, but if she did engage you in conversation, it was a frustrating experience, because you only ever heard half of what she wanted to say. Her breathing was very bad, and if she ran out of breath in the middle of a sentence, she would just keep mouthing away noiselessly till she had reached a full stop or filled her lungs again. She used quaint dialect words too. To her, ants were "emmets". Only once did I ever go into her cottage, when I was taken in by Ernie Gardiner, who used to keep an eye on her and help around her garden. I was shown into a dank old kitchen, where there was an ancient metal oven, into which I was told that boys would be put when they were naughty. This did not encourage me to return, especially once I became familiar with the story of Hansel and Gretel. Margey had a niece called Ivy, who was her only visitor. She was forever talking, and certainly made up for her aunt. My mother would say she had "a real clack on her". My father referred to her as "Poison Ivy".

Apart from the human residents of Rock Cottages there were two cats: Tibby Heaven, a mottled grey tabby, and our own Stumpy. Wishing to dissuade mice and worse after we had arrived at Rodborough, my father was persuaded by one of his workmates to take a "male Manx kitten". Stumpy turned out to be neither male, nor Manx, though she was a tiny black kitten whose tail had been docked, leaving a circular stump. She spent the first night asleep in my dad's slipper. Thereafter she had a rather hard life with us. My mother professed not to like cats, and tended to blame Stumpy for anything which went wrong, whether it was the state of the floor or a smell in the pantry. She said she resented the cost of the cat food, and she certainly resented the health hazard which Stumpy posed, for from time to time Stumpy would be afflicted with tape worms, egg-bearing segments of which would drop out of her rear end. Rarely, if ever, was she taken to the vets, it being much more affordable to treat her with patent medicines bought over the counter at the chemists'. For my own part, as a very young child, I was also less than kind to her. I would trap her behind an armchair and then sit in the chair forcing it back against the wall. When my parents asked me why I behaved like that, I replied: "'Cos I got to!"

On one occasion, Stumpy came home with her fur soaked through. My parents suspected somebody in the terrace had poured a bucket of water over her, though nothing was said. We then learned that Margey Bates was on the warpath (a curious image, given her limp), because a cat had stolen her fish from the bucket of water where she endeavoured to keep it fresh for her tea. For some reason, Tibby Heaven became the prime suspect and was duly punished. Again, nothing was said. Only then did it occur to us that Stumpy's drenching must have been the result of upsetting the bucket whilst making her get-away!

The Gardies themselves had no pet. (Why would they need one, when they had my sister!) But I recall their indulgent attitude to cats whom we wished to discipline, and indeed to any creature which had the misfortune to cross our path: "Let 'n bide. 'ee don' mean no 'arm. Let 'n bide!"

When we had been resident at Rock Cottages for a few years, the mature hedge opposite our cottages was ripped out and the field behind developed for three further houses: a tall grey house, which was purchased by the Chudleighs; a bungalow which was purchased by Mr Short, who promptly died, leaving a widow; and another bungalow behind hers, the name of whose owners was Peacey. I hardly ever spoke to Mrs Short, who seemed to spend her whole life doing the washing up at her kitchen window. The Chudleighs, however, we did get to know, especially once they had a little boy called Nicky, with whom my sister, Ros, and I would occasionally be allowed to play, until his mother decided that I was too rough!

Until I went to school, my world was really defined by my immediate family, the wider family whom I will describe later, and by the Rock Cottage neighbours. The only other individuals who impinged on that world were tradesmen who called with deliveries: Vernon the breadman, the coal man, the milkman, the little chap who sold vegetables from a van, the Corona man, the doctor, and a very few shopkeepers. (My mother would shop most days, but usually only at the Co-op, quite a way down Rodborough Hill, and at the post office store, which was at the crossroads a little below our cottages at "the Pike" and opposite the Prince Albert pub.) A trip into Stroud for a bigger shop was more of an event., which probably occurred no more than once a week.

CHAPTER 2

We moved to Rock Cottages in 1955 when I was two. Of my life before then, I have only the vaguest impressions. Once these may have been actual memories, but they now seem no more than memories of memories, or of black and white photographs of things I once knew.

In recollection, I am angry and distressed, because my parents have built some sort of barrier to stop me entering their tiny kitchen. (It is in the top floor flat they occupied at the White family home at 25 Lansdown in Stroud itself.) They seem amused that I am angry. I hate them.

In another, some friends of my parents, the Packfords, have come to visit. Their son, Andrew, and I play with the wooden casing for my mother's sewing machine. He chatters away, since he is older.

"Martin, why don't you talk like Andrew," they chide. I know I could, but I won't.

In a third vignette, we are having a meal at our bed and breakfast in Weston-super- Mare. It is my first ever holiday. The radio is on, and they are talking about shooting rabbits. At eighteen months old, why does my father try to explain myxomatosis to me?

Real photographic images do provide a route back into those years, both before and whilst we lived at Rodborough, but in fact there are so few: just two family albums for the years 1955-1962, bound in thick blue covers and in the landscape format standard in those days. It seems my parents would only take one or two films of perhaps 12 exposures each on their Box Brownie for each twelve-month period. There is also a smaller album – "a baby album" - with a grey cover, which is devoted to pictures of me. Most striking are the pictures of my christening, of which, of course, I have no recollection at all. There are flags and buntings flying, but they are not for me. They are for the Queen, who is about to be crowned.

Despite the general paucity of photographs, I have far more memories of the early years at Rodborough: memories which feel as though they lodge in my own bones, rather than mere glimpses of someone else's life projected upon a screen. My sister's birth, when I am four, stands out. My mother is ironing. Several times she bends forward, clutching her belly. She hurries me down to the phone box at the Pike, where I stand outside as she makes a call.

Then my mother is no longer present, but my father has come home from work, which is most unusual. The district nurse arrives, which **is** usual, but I tell her: "You're too late. She's gone!"

My father then takes me down to the post office shop in order to buy something for my dinner: Tom Thumb is on the tin, and I am deposited with Mrs Heaven, who will warm it up for me.

Some days later my father takes me to my grandparents' house in Horns Road, whilst he visits the nearby maternity hospital. When he returns, it is my grandmother's turn to scuttle along to see the new baby, but later, as my father and I walk down to the bus, Gran is standing outside the hospital wearing her "woe is me" face. They wouldn't let her in – only husbands are allowed to visit.

Finally, my sister is brought home to Rock Cottages, her carrycot is placed on the table and my parents ask me what I think of her. I am disappointed: I had been promised someone to play with, which, it is clear, she is not. Her name is Rosalind, but for a time I refer to her as "the Ros".

My sister was born in 1957: the year that I was first aware of the year as having a number. It was the year when I said to my mother, as she cleaned the rather attractive red-brick fireplace in the living room at 4 Rock Cottages: Just think, mummy, you've had me now for **FOUR** years!"

It was also the year when later I went to school for the first time.

Rodborough Infants' School was a long low building, which appeared to be built out of corrugated iron, though it was warm enough inside, each of its two classrooms having a cylindrical black charcoal burner, which the two teachers had to keep going in Winter. The school was located just over halfway down Rodborough Hill, behind a thick row of trees and hedges, and was adjacent to a Secondary Modern School. It was so close, in fact, that we infants to access our toilets we had to cross the teenagers' playground, though we rarely encountered them, because their playtimes and ours were different. Our own playground was a rectangular tarmacked area in front of our school, but at a slightly higher level, which meant that railings were necessary between the yard and the school buildings.

The day my mother took me down to be enrolled at the infants' school, I clung to her skirts as she wove her way among the desks in Miss Scott's classroom, before passing through a cloakroom reeking of carbolic, and on into a classroom for younger children over which Miss Bowering presided. In no time (is it a matter of minutes, days or weeks?) I am actually seated there as a pupil – the most junior on a table of six, being told by a rather motherly five-year-old called Mary that I must now learn my ABCs.

Miss Bowering remained my teacher for my full three years at the school. She was a small dumpy woman with glasses and dark hair, who seemed to know all there was to know about the natural world, and, in fact, spent so much time taking us on nature walks, that my parents worried I would never learn the basics of reading, writing, and arithmetic. In fairness, Miss Bowering and her teaching methods were not entirely to blame, for, if urged to do something in which I was not immediately interested, I would trot out my favourite mantra: "I'm not old enough to do that!"

I applied this to everything from my five times table to tying my shoelaces. In the end my parents took matters into their own hands and coached me to read "Janet and John" books at home in the evenings!

I had little to do with Miss Scott. She was elderly, emaciated and (as I now realise) unwell. She shuffled and her hands shook, so that, if she came to see Miss Bowering, you had good warning, because the handle of the classroom door would start to rattle under her grip before she made any entry into the room.

As far as the other pupils were concerned, a succession of little girls became my "girlfriend", one of whom, Sandra Frost, I kissed under the pine tree near the road, and another of whom, Susan Robbins, cut me to the quick when she said she no longer wanted to be my girlfriend or to play with me, because I was too rough! (That charge again!) Yet another, Lynn Gillingham, annoyed me by leaving the school when her parents moved to Gosport!

I found it more difficult to make friends with the little boys. (Indeed, I bemoaned to my Aunty Dorothy that I thought I would **never** be friends with one Harold Harris!) The other boys seemed obsessed with tv programmes, especially "Whirly Birds", which involved helicopters, and with "Steering" Moss who apparently was a racing driver. The boys would run around the playground making car and helicopter noises or, if the game involved "the Germans", the sound of machine-guns. We had neither a tv at 4 Rock Cottages, nor a car, and certainly not a racing car. However, these and other memories of the infant school seem cloaked in an antediluvian glow of well-being, rather than the more Spartan gloom of my next school.

There were, nevertheless, humiliations to be borne. On one occasion, Nicky Lear stole my plasticene, and so I chased him round the desks to get it back, only to be blamed for the incident and made to stand red-faced, ears burning, by the teacher's desk with my back to the classroom. Then there was the occasion when I had to own up that it was me who had put soiled toilet paper, not down the toilet pan, but in the space behind the privy; and it was, of course, me who then had to go and clean it up! Finally, there was that February day when, after a week or so's absence from school due to illness, it was time for me to return, although that very day (18th) was my mother's birthday! I went down the hill to school with great reluctance and very bad grace, and claimed to be poorly as soon as the class convened for singing. When I was allowed to go and stand in the carbolic cool of the cloakroom, out of the teacher's gaze, I immediately ran all the way back up the hill to see my mother's birthday cards. Before long Miss Bowering arrived, panting and complaining. As she spoke to my mother in our living room, I threw a slipper at her head! I was, nevertheless, allowed to stay home that morning, and, indeed, to go for a walk on the Common with Ernie Gardiner and my sister, who was in a pushchair; but when I returned to school that afternoon Miss Bowering made it very clear that such behaviour should never be repeated!

Two official photographs of pupils at Rodborough Infants' School, which I still retain, are slightly mysterious. One shows thirty children gathered round Father Christmas. (The inimical Harold Harris is smiling like a little angel at his elbow, whereas I am present only as a right ear protruding from behind the motherly Mary.) The other photograph shows thirty-five children in more formal rows between Miss Bowering in the top right-hand corner and Miss Scott in the top left. Many of the children I still recognise, to some I can put a Christian name, and to a few a surname as well. What is unclear is whether the photographs were intended to be of the whole school (or at least all of those who were present on the day the photographer called.) Certainly, there are children from the year above me (Brenda is included on both occasions), but there are also others whom I remember, but who are missing. Maybe the school really was so small that only thirty to forty children were pupils at one time, or maybe the school was divided roughly in two for the purpose of taking photographs.

Two other photographs of maybe a year later are of a Christmas party, one again featuring Father Christmas. In both I stand out as the one boy wearing dark clothes (blazer and short grey trousers) whilst everyone else is more casually dressed. I am also next to a girl called Wendy in both photographs. She was clearly my girlfriend for the time being.

The most important event in the infant school year was the Christmas concert and nativity play. I must have been involved in three, unless I was away ill one year. Whatever the case, I have recollections of only two. The first must have been at the end of my initial term, when I had to tell the Virgin Mary that I was a donkey and that I would give her a ride on my back. Of the other occasion, I remember little or nothing of the nativity play itself or of any other entertainments, but only the long slow climb up Rodborough Hill afterwards with my mother. I had what my mother always termed "neuralgia" in the face, and we had agreed that I was "sickening for something". Therefore, I felt fully justified in being whiney and tearful – even more so when we encountered a couple of dogs who were fighting. Whether from illness or fright, I managed to fall over in the gutter at the sight of them, only for them to continue their hostilities over my prostrate body till my mother managed to rescue me.

Apart from the nativity play, there were end-of-term tea parties run by Miss Bowering, which were typified by cakes and blancmanges of a far more bilious hue and sugariness than I had ever encountered at home; and every Friday afternoon in term time our sugar intake would also be topped up (just in time for a boisterous weekend) by the distribution to each child of five sweets from the voluminous handbag of an ancient and spindly spinster called Miss James, who lived in a Virginia creeper-clad Edwardian mansion on the corner of Queens Road and Coronation Road near our local bus stop. She was something of a patron of the school, ever-present at concerts and teas in thick blue coat and ankle-length skirts topped with a blue hat, which seemed to be made from plasticated straw and to be too far big for her.

When I first attended Rodborough Infants' School, my mother walked me there and back in the morning, at lunchtime, and after school. She could only do so if my sister was first lodged with the Gardies, which may well have accounted for how she became so very much a part of their household. Before too long, however, an older girl called June, who attended the secondary school and who lived in one of the lanes to the right of the Common as you ascended the hill above us, suggested to my mother that she could take charge of me each time the journey was made. I submitted to this change in my routine, though on occasions I complained that June walked too quickly for me to keep up, and so my mother had to have a little word with her every so often. Later there was a rather ugly incident when on a non-school day June called to take me up on to the Common with Ros in a pushchair. I do not think it was planned (certainly not by June), but on our walk we encountered some older girls who lived in the Spillmans, and we all sat around one of the public benches which were provided on the

Common. One of the girls was smoking and out of pure devilment wanted to see what would happen if she stubbed out a cigarette on my sister's hand. When we returned home, my mother found little burns on Ros' palms and, when I explained what had happened, this must have put an end to all association with older children, for I do not remember June after that. In the latter part of my time at the Infants' School I generally made the trip from The Butts to school and back again on my own, or with other infants with whom I was friendly. (Did I really tell Carole Powell all about my bed-wetting on one such occasion?)

I remained at Rodborough Infants' School until the Summer of 1960 when, at the age of seven and a half, I was due to progress to a junior school. There was a choice: between Church Street Boys', near the parish church of St Lawrence in Stroud, and a much smaller school at Kingscourt, a village quite close to Rodborough, just down from the southern flank of the Common. My mother vacillated. At first it was bound to be Church Street, because it had some sort of reputation, was attended by most boys in the area, and had been attended by her own brother, my Uncle Maurice. But it was nearly half an hour's walk from where we lived, part of the route being along the busy Bath Road and across several zebra crossings. So, when the mother of two of my friends, Paul and Geraldine Woolley, put the case for Kingscourt, with its rural setting and the irresistible attraction of her own children's presence there, my mother wavered and then re-registered me as a prospective pupil, only to start wavering again at the thought of the narrow wooded lane to Kingscourt, especially on dark Winter mornings, when strange men could be about. (There was clearly a distinction between strange men on the way to Kingscourt and any I might encounter going up and down Rodborough Hill!) In the end, after I was dragged along to a conference at Castle Street School in Stroud with Miss Caerleon, who seemed to be the senior headmistress for all infant schools in the immediate area, my mother chose the risk of traffic accidents over child abduction, and I was re-enrolled at Church Street from the following September.

CHAPTER 3

My parents were rather shy people. My father was quietly spoken, gentle and polite in his manner, though, if things went wrong, he tended to panic and exclaim: "Stone the crows!" He was given to self-denial, always taking the smallest helping of any cake or delicacy offered: he would always "make do". Consistent with this, my father had low self-esteem and was self-deprecating. Years later he would say to me: "Well, at least I made a success of my marriage and my family."

As if everything else in his life had been a failure!

My mother was a more decisive individual, and quite assertive within the immediate family. If she was with people she didn't know well, she would cover her feelings of inadequacy with a laughing breezy (slightly frenzied) exterior, whereas with those she did not know at all, she would be almost mute.

If I try to remember gestures which expressed something of their personalities, I see my father tugging his nose and slapping his thigh in embarrassed amusement – enjoying the moment, but unsure how to express it. I see my mother clasping her hands together, maybe rubbing them in a determined manner, maybe muttering conversations she was about to have: oblivious to what surrounded her. If she was reading the newspaper, you had to really shout to gain her attention.

If I think about the things they used to say, there were set expressions and phrases of which they were particularly fond. My mother was forever referring to "mother-of-pearl skies", my father to "switchback roads". Female singers were so often described as "a chicken peeing in an empty biscuit tin" – a phrase they had picked up from heaven knows what 50s radio comedy sketch. In later years, my father latched on to a description he always applied to Harold Wilson, which referred to his "regurgitating closet voice", whereas Cliff Richard was forever branded as having a "malted milk voice". Both of them would refer to "faded gentility", most often in relation to my father's family!

They were not demonstrative people. Whilst we children received a smattering at least of hugs and kisses, I never saw them embrace each other. In fact, one day (it must have been in the late 50s) my mother told me that they had decided that they ought to hug and kiss when my father came home from work! That day they did – but it was all treated as a joke, as if they were play-acting, and was not repeated. On another occasion, when during the previous evening Ros and I had been draping ourselves over our mother as she sat by the fire, my mother confided in us that she thought my father felt neglected at such times and we should hug him too. This we duly did, since this revelation filled me with guilt. You could say, though, that spontaneity and obvious affection were not the family's strongest suit! To this day I find myself sneering at the sight of a married couple holding hands.

My parents had married in 1949. On the sideboard at 4 Rock Cottages was a wooden biscuit barrel, a gift from the Stroud Choral Society, celebrating the event. Unfortunately, it recorded the nuptial date as 10 September 1949, whereas in fact it had been two days earlier. My parents, being the people they were, had never wanted to embarrass anyone by pointing out the mistake. We had photographs of their wedding too, of course, but only a few. My father looked debonair – at times he could resemble Laurence Olivier, though by then he had shaved off the thin moustache. My mother and her friend, our Aunty Joan Taylor (as bridesmaid), were in white lacy-looking dresses and veils, though cut to just below the knee, rather than proliferating in costly flounces and trains. An army friend of my dad's (later to be my godfather), Les Harmer, was best man.

My father was then twenty-nine, my mother twenty-eight: quite old, you might think, but, of course, there had been The War. My father (and presumably Les Harmer) had been in North Africa, Palestine and Italy. My mother had worked shifts at Hoffman's, the ball-bearing manufacturers near Stonehouse. After the war my father had spent some time in London, learning and then teaching tap-dancing. They had not, in consequence, met until a matter of months before they married.

The War seemed to be the backdrop and explanation of so many things which occurred in my childhood. Apart from its re-enactments in the schoolyard, and the role it played in stories my mother used to tell me (the air raids, the rationing, the blackout), it was such a feature of the tv. Once my parents had decided that I must be feeling disadvantaged at school, where "Whirlybirds" so dominated playground games, they purchased a second-hand tv set. Very soon we became addicted to the endless war films, of course, but also to "The Valiant Years": a multi-episode account of the Second World War, broadcast every Saturday evening, and featuring the voice of Richard Burton as Winston Churchill.

Up until the arrival of a tv in 1960, most of my entertainment had been provided by the radio. My parents possessed a rather handsome wireless set, which sat on one of the shelves to the right of the red-brick grate. In due course, I was to discover that it could provide the delights of S1, S2, and S3, but for the time being life revolved around the Light Programme and Home Service. The former provided what I at first termed "my crogramme" ("Listen with Mother"), which came on after the "Shilling Forecast". As I became older, I turned more to the Light Programme's "Children's Favourites" with Uncle Mack on Saturday mornings and to "Children's Hour" with David Davis daily on the Home Service. Particular names still resonate: "Norman and Henry Bones", "The Children of Blowy Tump", "Phra the Phoenician", "Windwhistle Farm" and "The Hobbit". Of adult programmes, I always listened to "Mrs Dale's Diary" with my mother when I came home from school and was eating jam sandwiches, but I also recall "Music While You Work", "Two Way Family Favourites" (with Jean Metcalf and Bill Crozier), "Workers' Playtime", "The Billy Cotton Band Show", and even an adaptation of "Lorna Doone" which had "By the Banks of Green Willow" as its theme music.

When the tv itself arrived, it was an impressive piece of furniture, standing in the corner of the living room between the front window and the sideboard. It had polished wooden doors which opened outwards to reveal an eighteen-inch screen. When you plugged it in, it would take some time to warm up and produce an image.

When it was purchased for £10 (after my mother saw an advertisement in the post office), it was not the first tv I had seen, for my grandparents and my dad's middle sister, Aunty Alice, had previously succumbed to what my parents at first affected to consider a modern frivolity, harmful to social and family life – at least until they decided to purchase one themselves. We had duly been taken – almost ceremonially - to view the sets owned by the relatives, and I remember having been terrified by a moray eel featured on a nature programme at Aunty Alice's, and bored by "Rag, Tag and Bobtail" and "Andy Pandy" at my Gran's. In addition, in the months before our own tv was purchased, our neighbours had obtained televisions too, and the Gardies had taken to inviting our whole family round to see such programmes as "The Black and White Minstrel Show", "The Ken Dodd Show", "Double Your Money", "Take Your Pick", "Life Begins at 80", "What's My Line" and "This is Your Life". Both sets of neighbours had also taken particular pity on my sister and me, to the extent that each evening, when the tv children's programmes came on, my sister would scamper round to the Gardies, whilst I would race round to the Heavens' especially to see "Popeye". (Their tv was usually tuned to TWW – South Wales and the West, rather than the BBC.) This was another reason my parents felt they could no longer resist the tide of popular culture.

Some months after we had obtained a tv, both sets of neighbours became addicts of "Coronation Street". "They be people like we!" Edie Gardiner would opine, in an attempt to persuade my parents to join the millions of other viewers. But my parents felt this was not the sort of thing we should be watching on our own set! Again it took them several years to catch on.

Once we had our own tv, visits to view programmes next-door (on both sides) diminished considerably. We honed our own taste in programmes, and once I had outgrown "Whirlybirds", mine tended to cartoons and puppet shows, such as "Supercar", "Fireball XL5", "Stingray", "The Flintstones" and "Top Cat" (which the BBC persisted in referring to as "Boss Cat" for fear of being accused of advertising cat food!) We did, of course, also watch Sunday tea-time dramatisations, such as "The Old Curiosity Shop" and "Oliver Twist", plus the children's magazine programme, "Blue Peter".

The living room which the tv came to dominate was at the front of No 4 Rock Cottages to the right of the front door as you went in. It occupied the corner of the ground floor at the very end of the terrace. In each outer wall was a window with an inset seat. I spent many hours standing on the seat in the front wall, which gave views across the Stroud Valley to Swift's Hill. I used to follow the flocks of pigeons which caught the sun as they wheeled above the railway station. I had to be dissuaded from staring across at Mrs Short on the day after her husband died. During Winter those windows would be thickly covered and patterned by frost until well into the day.

At the opposite end of the room from the front window and tv was the red brick fireplace on which my mother lavished so much attention, but which was not very efficient as a grate, since smoke used to billow out into the sitting room when the wind was in the wrong direction (which was most of the time). It might be supplemented by a two-bar electric fire, which was placed in front of it. Not appreciating the difference between coal and electricity, my little sister was once prevented at the very last moment from prodding the electric fire with a metal poker! On either side of the fireplace there were sets of shelves and cupboards let into the walls, those on the left occupied by plates, books, ornaments and my toys; those on the right by the wireless, more ornaments, more books, an ancient gramophone and a pile of seventy-eights. Opposite the room's other window (which overlooked Rock View) was the glass-panelled door out into the hallway, which led from the front to the back of the house.

As for the contents of the living room, they comprised two armchairs either side of the grate, a sofa at the opposite end of the room in front of the front window, the sideboard with the biscuit barrel (and also within it a small drinks cabinet), and an extending dining table with four chairs – all of them "utility ware", which my mother said was all they could get when they were first married, and for which she expressed distaste, though in retrospect they were solid, consistent in style, and lasted us many years. The floor was of stained wooden boards, the majority of which was covered with linoleum – so cold under bare feet! Those areas of the lino which were free of furniture would rise, hover and fall, depending on the strength of the draught from outside or from the cellar below!

There was a large mirror over the fireplace and a mantelpiece on which was a clock, together with brass candlesticks and brass ornaments made from First World War munitions. The room also contained two reproduction pictures: Hobbema's "Avenue" to the right of the door as you came in, and a Dutch master with a young woman delivering a letter to an older woman to its left. This picture had a slight scuff mark on it caused by a projectile slipper (though not, I believe, the one directed at Miss Bowering!) My father's interest in art was reflected in the book collection either side of the grate. It contained various volumes devoted to individual artists, but also a rather fat book which covered the whole of Western Art from the Roman Period onwards. I used to leaf through this – mainly to see all the naked bodies - but nevertheless gaining a notion of art history in the process.

Moving out of the living room and into the hallway, the front door had frosted glass panels, one of which I had occasion to crack with a pudding spoon. One Sunday lunchtime my father had told me that, unless I behaved and ate up, he would go down to the phone box to tell Father Christmas not to call that year. When he strode out of the front door, apparently with this evil purpose in mind, I smote the glasswork with my pudding spoon with all the force a six-year-old could muster. Later I told the glazier who came to repair it: "I did that when I was tempered!"

The hallway itself was characterful: my father had lined the damp walls with hardboard and had painted everything canary yellow! From the front door it skirted to the right of the stairs, then, once the stairs were out of the way, veered left and proceeded through a broader section which contained in the floor a trapdoor down to the cellar. It ended at the pantry, at which point, if you turned right, you went down a step into the kitchen. Under the stairs was a cupboard containing cleaning materials and, occasionally, mice. Our cat, Stumpy, was once deliberately locked in to catch one of them, only to be let out a couple of hours later pursued by her intended quarry!

The cellar, which was accessed from the hallway, was a place of fear and trepidation: unlit and musty smelling, it was almost like a cave and had an earthen floor. Its main use was as a coal store, the coal being poured through a smaller trap door located outside the living room window at the front of the house. At one point my father became enthused with plans for an alternative use for the cellar: mushroom growing! He purchased special compost, wooden plant boxes and bales of hay, only to find (or so he claimed) that he would also have to irrigate the mushrooms by flooding the cellar itself, and, since the house was already severely affected by damp, he decided against proceeding. The hay later proved invaluable when it came to stuffing the bodies of a succession of Guy Fawkeses.

The pantry at the end of the hallway was a small square room with its own window, itself divided into small, square (and probably quite ancient) leaded panes, giving on to the back of the house. It had a floor of Marley red tiles, various shelves, which housed utensils, but also rusks and biscuits (the latter in a tin whose lid showed a galleon under sail), and most memorably the meat safe, which had been painted blue and had an unpleasant smell of lamb fat. Eventually, not long before we moved from the property, its place was usurped by my parents' second modern purchase: a small refrigerator.

Rather than enter the pantry when you reached the end of the hallway, you would more frequently turn right into the kitchen. In proportion to the rest of the house, the kitchen was quite large. Again, it had a red Marley floor, and across this you could reach the back door, which, by way of a steep step down, took you to the pathway which ran along the backs of the cottages from Margie Bates' to Rock View.

At the far end of the kitchen was a large sink with a draining board, cupboards beneath and an Ascot (our only, and rather inefficient, means of obtaining hot water). The kitchen sink was where my hair was washed periodically. I would stand on a chair and lean over the basin, whilst my parents soaped and rinsed my hair to my own enormous distress – assuaged only in part when my soapy hair was shaped into two horns, and I was told to look in the mirror and see how I had become a "moo cow". To the right of the basin was a window, the top pane of which was usually open and afforded access (at least to a child of my proportions) when the back door key had been forgotten. In front of it was the boiler for doing the washing and, in particular, nappies, once my sister had arrived.

Apart from that, the kitchen possessed a cream-coloured gas cooker, a table with a couple of chairs, a long low bench (on which you sat to clean your shoes), a mangle, and a tall kitchen cabinet with a drop down front to provide a working surface. Its upper cupboards had glass panels, one of which had been cracked and was held together with aging Sellotape. Apparently, I was responsible for this breakage too, having thrown a child's building brick at it for who knows what reason. Perhaps the threatened non-appearance of Father Christmas was again to blame. So, Miss Bowering's head, the Dutch letter painting, the glass of the front door and the kitchen cabinet were united in having attracted my ire.

The kitchen was my mother's domain, and necessarily so. In the late 50s and early 60s much of a housewife's day was monopolised by laundry duties and cooking. With no washing machine and no dryer, Monday and quite probably Tuesday, (maybe even Wednesday) of each week would be taken up with soaking pillowcases in Robin's starch, hand-washing and boiling bedding and clothes for four people, squeezing it all through the mangle and, when eventually it had dried outside on the washing-line, with ironing it and then airing it in front of the living room fire, or later in the "Flatley", as recommended by Mrs Heaven (modern acquisition No 3). The bedding alone would have been a demanding chore, especially since my sister was very small and I, as Carole Powell now knew, was an inveterate bed-wetter - almost until adolescence. Sheets would therefore need washing throughout the week. Apart from the occasional, "What have I done to deserve it?", when she threw back my bedclothes in the morning, I don't remember my mother ever complaining about this situation, and this was even though the continual rounds of washing rendered her hands red raw and split in Winter. ("Spreedy 'ans", as my grandmother used to call them). In Winter also the sheets would become frozen stiff on the washing line and would have to be manhandled by my mother up the circuitous garden path and back to the kitchen.

In fact, despite her chores, my mother often seemed at her happiest in the kitchen, for she would sing loudly and very tunefully whilst she worked. Her one ambition in life had been to be a singer, but she had never progressed beyond the occasional local competition, singing contralto with the Stroud Choral Society (under the direction of one

Charlie Ferris), roles in operetta at the Stroud Subscription Rooms, and duets (such as "All in an April Evening") with my godmother, Aunty Joan Taylor, which they performed at old folks' homes around the Stroud Valleys. Her repertoire was therefore comprised of songs mainly from the 30s and 40s, Gilbert and Sullivan (she had been a Little Maid), and Handel (whose "Messiah" she adored). Her singing could be heard throughout the house, and outside too, so much so that Mrs Heaven would often compliment her.

She would also spend much time cooking. I seem to remember "dinner" being served in the middle of the day, but there was also the need for an evening meal for my father when he came home from work. The main meals of a typical week would have been Roast on Sunday (lamb or beef), followed by apple pie (my mother's own) or lemon meringue pie (from a Mary Baker packet); cold meat and chips on Monday; stew with dumplings (to which my father would add raw curry powder) on Tuesday; maybe mincemeat and potato pie on Wednesday; Shepherd's Pie on Thursday; sausages or a fry-up on Friday; and faggots and peas on Saturday. Then there was breakfast (usually something cooked, even if only a boiled egg or ReadyBrek); tea at 4.15, featuring bread and jam (and on Sundays often bread and dripping or sandwiches made with Shiphams salmon or chicken paste); and eventually supper (cornflakes, tinned soup or bread and Bovril) before bed. Over the years there was a shift towards more convenience food, such as beefburgers, fishfingers, and steaklets. When we were introduced to yoghurt, we decided that one small pot was enough for all of us, since we used it solely as an adornment for a bowl of cereal (one spoonful each)!

My mother's forté was, however, baking pastry and cakes, both of which in retrospect we seem to have devoured in huge quantities. (The household consumption of sugar, and of the fatty substance called Trex, which my mother swore by, was phenomenal.) That said, I was a difficult child where food was concerned and, though I would eat puddings and cakes, I had no interest in main meals, preferring only chips ("tips") and jam. My mother became rather desperate, especially when her own father's exhortation to "get 'n get it down ya," failed.

She would try to encourage me to eat by inventing stories about the meals she placed in front of me, so that, for instance, sausages became giants, chips their building materials, and peas their projectile weapons when fighting each other! She also took me to the doctor, who only said: "Look at his bonny thighs – He's not malnourished. He's getting it from somewhere, so stop worrying!"

But she did worry, and eventually decided, like so many parents at that time, that the answer lay in my tonsils. It had to be that I wasn't eating, because my tonsils were diseased and were depriving me of all sense of taste! The doctor gave in, she had her way, and in January 1960 I was to undergo surgery.

Occasionally, my mother would let me help her with her various chores in the kitchen (at least until I became bored). Mixing cakes (and licking the mixing bowl) was one example, but also, if she was doing the ironing, she would disconnect the iron and then allow me to iron handkerchiefs as it cooled down. When I had finished, she would say: "I couldn't have done it better myself," which I loved to hear, and which set up a strange yardstick by which I measured myself, even very much later in life, when I would often check with myself whether I was doing whatever I was doing better than my mother could have done!

She did try to interest me in knitting and corking (which involved the wooden centre of a cotton reel into which four small nails had been hammered, a lot of old wool and a safety pin, and which produced a long, thin knitted tube, which itself could be formed into place mats and such like!) I did attempt these things, but never had sufficient patience to perfect any skill. My mother, of course, was an inveterate knitter, continually producing jumpers and cardigans. She could hardly bear to listen to the radio or watch the tv without the continual accompaniment of her clicking needles!

CHAPTER 4

The main staircase at 4 Rock Cottages began a few feet behind the front door, and up its middle ran a thin floral carpet with painted woodwork on either side. At the top it joined a narrow passage which led towards the back of the house. That was where my own bedroom was located. It contained my single bed in front of a blocked-up grate, a chunky chest of drawers, and some wooden boxes housing more toys. On several occasions our parents moved a second bed in for my sister to use, but she was never happy with this arrangement and would cry so loudly and for so long that soon her bed would be moved back to our parents' room.

Their bedroom, opposite the top of the stairs, was of a fair size – roughly the size of the living room immediately below. It was at the front of the house, and, like the living room, had casement windows and window seats in its two outer walls. The furnishings comprised a utility-ware double-bed, dressing-table, small wardrobe (my father's) and big wardrobe (my mother's); at first, my sister's cot; and later (for most of the time) her bed.

One Summer evening in the early '60s, when Ros and I had gone to bed and should have been trying to fall asleep, we were romping about on her bed and making a lot of noise, when, to our surprise, our parents did not come up to stop us. The reason was that they were making so much noise themselves: bellowing with laughter at what turned out to be the first episode (perhaps the pilot) of "Steptoe and Son"!

The one bathroom in the house was also situated on the first floor, but it was in the far corner of the building behind (and only accessible through) my bedroom. This meant that to use the facilities family members and the occasional guest would have to enter my bedroom, even if I was there asleep. It contained a bath, a sink and a toilet. Its frosted window faced Rock View.

Even such meagre bathroom facilities were a privilege compared with those enjoyed by our neighbours and by some of our relatives. Neither the Heavens, the Gardies, nor indeed my grandparents had bathing facilities (other than an old tin bath). Nor did any of them have an internal loo. The daily wash would have been performed at the kitchen sink at Rock View and at my grandparents' house, and in "the glory hole" (a sort of scullery off the kitchen) at No 3. It seemed unlikely Margey Bates had use for washing facilities of any description. She did, though, have an outside loo near her backdoor – a place into which I never ventured – and the Heavens and Gardies each had adjacent outside loos at the end of Margey's garden. The Heavens' loo was a bit dark and damp-feeling and had a reddish-brown door. The Gardies' was painted cream throughout and had a conical "pan" set in a broad wooden seat - all behind a green latched door. As I lay in bed at night, I would often hear the clank of a water-bucket as one or other of the Gardies walked past our back door and under my bedroom window on their way to relieve themselves. None of the outside loos had running water.

As for our own ablutions, these involved a wash at the bathroom sink in the morning, though my father would also wash when he came home from work. For me, a wash really meant face, hands, and perhaps feet, though if I had wet the bed, it went further. My mother used to wash my private parts and would say: "Oh! What a specimen!" which made me laugh, once she had explained what "specimen" meant.

Baths took place on Sundays, and the poor old Ascot had to labour to meet the demands of my parents and myself, all before Sunday lunch, and then heat enough water for the after-lunch washing-up as well. (Whilst she was very small, my sister was bathed in a little enamelled bath in front of the fire every evening.) Why we did not stagger our baths over several days (especially since we each only had one bath a week) I cannot imagine, except that bathing on Sunday was as immutable a feature of our routine as was doing the main clothes washing on Monday.

The first floor was not the end of the matter as far as the layout and contents of our house were concerned. If you turned right at the top of the stairs, the narrow unlit passageway dog-legged past my parents' bedroom and continued towards the front of the house, where you came to a door on the right giving access to another flight of wooden steps (uncarpeted) up to the attic: a place of mouldy smells, muddles, and beams full of woodworm.

Fairly early in our time at Rodborough, my parents had had a small bedroom installed at one end of the attic, just to your right as you reached the top of the stairs. In context, this felt modern and bright and smelled of paint and fresh wood. It was the only part of the attic to have any wall covering or paint at all, even if the floor was of bare stained wood. Apart from a single bed, it contained nothing other than my father's typewriter, which balanced on the windowsill. The room was primarily intended as a guest room and was used in particular by my mother's brother, Maurice, when my grandparents were away away on holiday. My father's youngest sister, Nancy, also stayed there on one occasion; and when I became eight or nine, I myself took up residence for a whole Summer, presumably whilst my parents tried to persuade my sister to sleep in my usual, as opposed to their, bedroom. I had up till then always been scared of the attic, its odours, and feeling of dereliction, but somehow relocating to its tiny bedroom seemed an adventure, which, for a while, I was happy to undertake. One night, however, I woke up with a sudden childhood fever, which startled me so much when I thought about it next morning that I moved back to the first floor immediately and for good.

The central and most decrepit room in the attic was next to the bedroom. It had no window, no electric light, no furniture and no floor covering. It did have dust and woodworm, and some of the beams and supports had to be replaced when the bedroom was constructed. Previously, my father had shown me chunks of beam which had fallen from the roof to the floor, simply eaten away and crumbling.

You hurried through that room as quickly as you could to get to a small door in the far corner, which led to the attic's final room, which had a more pleasant feel, partly because it had a window and daylight. It contained the house's water tank, but otherwise was used only for storing oddments mainly associated with my father. It was there that the bales of straw intended as part of the abortive mushroom –growing experiment were kept. So too was my father's make-up box - he was a keen amateur actor - and also boxes of tap-dancing shoes!

When my father had been demobbed after the Second World War he had avoided being sucked into the White Family's small printing business at 23 George Street, and had gone to London to teach tap-dancing (whilst living at the YMCA). I have no idea how or why he had become skilled on the dancefloor, but it proved his means of escape, albeit briefly. Within a couple of years, however, his father had prevailed on him to return to help rescue "John White, Printers", which by then was beginning to fail. It was at that point that he met my mother. Once they were married, he'd had to settle down and in due course forget the dancefloor altogether. (My mother had no skills as a dancer, and had no intention of obtaining any.)

It was in that tiny room that my father would do oil painting and other artistic things, like annually creating our Guy Fawkes, which he would embellish with sequins from his make-up box, so that its eyes glinted as the flames took hold! Though he also wrote poetry, I doubt that much, if any, was written in this room, which had no table. I certainly never came across any of his poems dating from those years at Rodborough, though I have a few from his army years, a smattering from the time after we had left Rodborough, and a small collection from the short years of his retirement.

Another association between my father and that small attic room: once, as I was standing in front of Mrs Heaven's house, I watched with alarm as he climbed out of its rickety old window and balanced on the ancient and equally rickety gutter (two storeys up!) in order to inspect the condition of the roof! He had no fear of heights and possessed the excellent balance of a dancer.

The roof and chimney were, in fact, in an increasingly perilous state, and eventually in the early 60s my father employed a builder to replace the chimney and repair the tiles. During the works there was one night a terrific storm, which caused the scaffolding to bang and clatter against the building and the still in situ old chimney. My parents were so frightened that the whole structure would come crashing through the roof that we all huddled for safety by the fireplace in the living-room until the storm subsided.

My father's artistic bent had meshed well with my mother's own interests when they were first married. I was told that they had met at a function at the Stroud Subscription Rooms, when one of them had said to the other: "Do you know Olive Darke?"

I never found out who Olive Darke was.

The Subscription Rooms had been the hub of Stroud's cultural activity at the time, and it was there that my mother had appeared in singing competitions and where her choir often performed. It was there also that, once they were married, my parents together participated in a number of Gilbert and Sullivan productions, my mother singing, my father singing and dancing, though neither in particularly major roles. The situation was different where amateur drama was concerned. My mother never participated, but my father was quite the star, both with the Trinity Players (where he was the lead in "Tobias and the Angel" – the photos show him in a loincloth and an horrendous wig!) and at the more prestigious Cotswold Playhouse situated at the top of the town. There he was Mole in "Wind and the Willows" and the lead (playing far younger than his actual age) in "How Green Was My Valley" -

"Obviously type-cast from the Rhondda," as an audience member was heard to announce.

I was taken to the former production, but, I regret, not the latter. I was also taken to see him in "Reluctant Heroes", during the course of which I shouted: "Why Daddy put his voice like that, eh? Why Daddy put his voice like that?"

Again, however, my father's theatrical escape from life as a printer was eventually curtailed, and this occurred once my sister was born. At that point, my mother decided, not unreasonably, that it was unfair for her to be left at home night after night looking after the children, whilst her husband trod the boards. So, my father, whose ability to deny himself pleasure was a defining characteristic, gave up his stage pursuits too. When, many years later, he retired from work and went back to amateur drama, he could not remember lines, and this seemed to obliterate his acting talent. Again, my mother bided her time, then prevailed upon him to stop.

As far as the later '50s and early '60s were concerned, my father's revolt against his lot in life was confined to occasional painting and drawing, collecting art books, and attempts to write short stories (such as one he began to type but never finished about one of my cuddly toys – a fair furred cat called Arthur White after my grandfather). He also had the odd harmless affectation, such as taking the occasional pinch of snuff, and sprinkling raw curry powder on his stew!

For all that he was by nature artistic, this did not prevent his efforts to be practical about the house. He undertook all decorating, though helped by my mother when it came to papering, and he endeavoured to deal with some of the rather damp and crumbly internal walls of the house by bolting panels of hardboard on to them. Joins were then taped over and the whole surface painted. By this method we acquired our canary yellow hallway. He laboured hard at improving the house, often in poor light after he came home from work; sometimes in hot weather stripped down to his rather ancient and strangely fleecy bathing trunks. If the results sometimes lacked finesse, even my mother would never have said so.

He was also scrupulous about the family's finances. Every Thursday night, after receiving the week's pay packet, he would take a large metal box from his wardrobe. It had various compartments and was kept locked. He would do his sums and allocate what he could to the various sections of the box, which related to things like electricity, gas, holidays and so on. I am sure he consulted my mother about such matters, but, though my mother had an excellent head for figures - years later she would go back to work as an accounts clerk - it was not until she was widowed that she grappled first hand with household budgets and paying bills: such had been my parents' conception of the roles within a marriage.

The printer's life against which my father was forever rebelling, either entirely, by going to London, or, once back in Stroud, by counter-balancing it with more congenial pursuits, such as acting and painting, was something to which he had been destined from birth. Both his father (Arthur Wilfrid White) and grandfather (John White) had run a printing business from an upstairs office almost opposite the Subscription Rooms. "John White, Printers" had dealt in small orders –

the trivia which people needed printing (party invitations, hymn sheets, vanity projects and the like) - far removed from the worlds of newspaper and book publishing. There had been the occasional commission of more substance. (For many years my father retained a copy of a book of poems which the firm had produced and which had been written by a local girl called June Hills, who had shown promise, but died young. It was entitled "Fragment", and inside there was a black and white photograph of June sitting on Rodborough Common. I do not know if or how well he knew her.) It was to this rather paltry business that my father returned in the late '40s, and he remained shackled to it until in due course his own father died, and it became obvious the business was all but bankrupt and would have to be wound up.

I am not quite sure at what point the business came to an end. Old Wilfy died in 1951. In 1955 my father was both working elsewhere and able to take out a mortgage on 4 Rock Cottages for most of the purchase price of £850. It seems likely, therefore, that "John White, Printers" closed not later than 1953, the year of my birth. And yet, I have a distinct memory of standing at the office window of 23 George Street beside my mother watching the arrival of Sir Anthony Eden to give a speech at the Subscription Rooms before the 1955 general election. Perhaps the business folded long before the property was sold or surrendered.

With the family business failing, there was no employment to which my father could turn, other than elsewhere within the printing industry, and, to use my mother's phrase, "he had to go cap in hand to the unions" to obtain an exemption from the usual apprenticeship qualifications required to work as a type-setter (which was the main professional skill he possessed). Against this background, he took a job on the local newspaper – "The Stroud News and Journal". Then, not long after we took up residence at Rodborough, he moved on to Baileys at Dursley. (I remember standing with my mother and Aunty Joan Taylor at my bedroom window at Rodborough trying to spot his bus home crossing the escarpment of Selsley Hill). Then he moved to a small printers' in the centre of Stroud (Collins'). He settled at neither, and the pay was poor. The figure of £5 a week was mentioned once in my hearing, as my mother emptied the last couple of coppers left before pay-day into her "Christmas Fund".

In 1960, however, my father moved to another newspaper to take up the job he was to carry out for 25 years (the remainder of his working life), and this was at "The Gloucester Citizen". If Bailey's had involved a bus ride to and from Dursley every day, working in Gloucester involved a significantly longer journey. Gloucester was the big city – way out in the Severn Valley, beyond Painswick and the Cotswold Hills. The work schedules at "The Citizen" meant that my father would from now on have Sundays off, plus one other day in the week: Tuesday one week, Wednesday the next, and so on. The weeks when he was home on Saturdays were therefore rare, though when they did occur he was entitled to a "long weekend", which included Monday as well; yet the following week he would have no day off at all.

Even at "The Citizen" he cannot have felt settled, for my parents at least thought about further moves whilst we still lived at Rodborough. At one point, my father's army friend, John Packford, suggested that he join a printing business he had set up at Oxford. At another, moving to a newspaper in Hastings was under contemplation. As for Oxford, my parents decided they would not wish to be "beholden to John", and as for Hastings, they (or at least my mother) could not accept being so far from my grandparents. In both instances "the children's schooling" was an additional consideration. With regard to Hastings, they also received representations from other relatives along the lines of "What about poor Allie" (meaning my father's sister, Alice) "left on her own in Stroud", which was a bit rich, since the relatives concerned had themselves long ago moved away to Norfolk!

CHAPTER 5

At first, I did not play much with my sister, mainly because of the four year age difference. A little later we would play independently, though in the same space - usually the living room - she with her model zoo, I with my model farm or fort. As we grew older, however, we did manage to devise games together. One in particular involved me on my hands and knees as the horse, Harriods, and Ros would sit astride my back as in our imaginations we crossed the Wild West and had various adventures, mainly invented by Ros. When we were in one or other of the bedrooms, we had another game which involved more raucous fun. She had various pairs of knickers, three of which were dyed an unattractive shade of brown. She christened them Eddie, Joe and Pete, and the game was for her to throw each one in turn at me, with the objective of landing one on my head. I would then reciprocate.

These self-invented games, particularly when a scatological element was included, were a lot more fun than playing with the various toys and gadgets which were bought for us by our parents and relatives to occupy our time. My sister never had a great interest in dolls, though she had a sizeable collection. We both had cuddly toys, but they seemed ornamental more than anything else. Plasticine and crayons would divert us, but only for a few minutes at a time. When later I was given airfix models (in which I had no interest at all) I dutifully stuck them together and then forgot about them. I similarly went through the motions in constructing two or three Meccano and Bayco structures. (Bayco was a system of assembling model houses or other buildings using metal rods stuck into a plastic base on to which plastic squares representing sections of wall could be slotted. Uncle Maurice spent money on a number of different sets of Bayco, without my ever demonstrating any aptitude of liking for the technology – for which my mother of course reproached me.) How much better it was to pretend to be a horse or to throw knickers about the room!

Out of doors I spent much time playing with Roger and Brenda, and sometimes Ros would join in too, though she was most frequently round with the Gardies. During evenings after school, it was likely that both Roger and Brenda would be available to play, though probably neither if it was any time on a Sunday, which was a family day. On

Saturdays, it would be just one of them, because the other would have been taken by their mother to help on her bread round. Delivering bread to the various villages in the Stroud Valleys and surrounding hills was Jean's employment for the whole period we lived at Rodborough.

One set of family photographs shows all four children rather impressively dressed up as pirates, no doubt assisted by my father's make-up box and a skill he had for adapting bits of cloth and clothing way beyond their original purpose. Others show Brenda and me playing at tea parties on the shady "lawn" at the front of our house, though there seem to be more of us doing the washing up afterwards! My sister is pictured too, wearing a little nurse's outfit, or pushing a doll's pram. In another, I am wearing my Red Indian outfit.

One Summer my mother organised a competition between the four of us - a competition to grow the biggest sunflower on the strip of garden furthest from the house. She provided the seeds, Roger and Brenda for some reason applied a lot of lime to their plants, and ultimately Roger won. Thereafter the strip became my own garden, and rather than suffer the indignity of losing further such competitions, I decided to devote it entirely to strawberries, once Ernie had given me one little bush to start off with.

Most time with Roger and Brenda was spent in the area behind Rock View, where there was another small lawn, but one which was much bigger and sunnier than our own. There were some flower borders and a rather ugly home-made wooden seat, intended principally for Stella when she felt like sun-bathing. In later years, I do remember very specific things we did there: looking at "Look and Learn" with Roger, whilst sitting on the garden bench, (leading to my first acquaintance with the concept of tectonic plates!); playing doctors and nurses on the lawn, with me as the patient and Ros again in her nurse's outfit; playing a game with Brenda and my sister, where I was "foreign" and spent my whole time speaking gobbledegook; one Summer looking after a tortoise, which Roger and I had found in the nearby fields and which took up residence under the garden seat until the Summer holidays came to an end and we had to shoo it through the hedge. (This proved sensible, because it then took up residence with Mr Cotterell, one of the neighbours who lived just down the bank).

That was not the only reptilian experience I associate with the Heavens' lawn. One Summer's day Tibby Heaven brought home a dead snake, which he deposited on the grass. Stella Heaven, who was of a nervous disposition and, in fact, would lock herself in the pantry with a candle, if thunder ever threatened, could not endure its presence, so Tom went to fetch Ernie, who was the resident expert on mice, rats and other vermin. Ernie approached the snake with his pitchfork, whilst I, together with Edie and Stella, stood at the side of the lawn to watch. Egged on by Tom, Ernie picked up the snake on his fork and threw it at us, at which point the snake came back to life and thrashed about as it descended towards our legs. Stella screamed and ran. I know I did too!

Some of our games took a more sinister turn, even without the intervention of Ernie and his pitchfork. Maybe because he lacked a father figure, Roger had a keen interest in authority, crime and its punishment. He was forever being the policeman, handcuffing us and taking us to prison. Often his games with me revolved around building prison-like mazes out of toy bricks, and then putting a woodlouse in the centre. If it made its way out, it would be released. If within an allotted time it did not, it would have to be executed. A toy canon would be loaded with a matchstick, and this would be fired in such a way as to decapitate the woodlouse. To my mother's ire, Roger went too far when one evening he decided that I was guilty of some crime or other and needed to be hanged. He and Brenda tied a string round my neck, braced it against the corner of Rock View and pulled hard, but they were not very skilled at tying knots. When later my mother found sore marks round my neck, and extracted the cause from me, she went round to complain! Corporal punishment ensued!

In later years (post 1960) our play was not restricted to the area immediately around the cottages. In a period considered far safer for children than nowadays, there were several places our parents were relaxed about allowing us to visit unsupervised: the Rectory Gardens, the fields, and the Common.

If you went a couple of hundred yards down Rodborough Hill, you came to what was known as The Pike. (There must have been a Turnpike there at some time, but nothing visible remained – which was not true, if you went east along Butterow Lane, where you would eventually come to an old Turnpike building, with an ancient sign advertising the turnpike rates.) Our Pike was where the hill's descent levelled out for maybe fifty yards between the Prince Albert Pub and the small shop/post office, which was opposite and which was run by a jovial couple, Elsie and Les Stockwell, who had a considerable array of tinned food, a fresh food counter, and an enormous circular blade for slicing sweet-smelling ham (and, it was again alleged, naughty boys!).

If you turned left at The Pike, you began the more gentle descent of Walkley Hill, past Rodborough Boulevard (where in the 80s there was to be a notorious and unsolved murder), and then past the Rectory Gardens. If you went on you would pass a lane off to the parish church on the right. This wound round the frontage of the old Endowed School, which only many years later I came to realise had a very attractive seventeenth century exterior. It contained firstly the Mother and Baby Clinic, where we used to take Ros to be weighed and injected with things, and secondly the Sunday School, which I was happy to attend as an infant, but which I came to hate when I was put into a more senior class presided over by a bossy 13 year old girl, who expected me to know everything which she herself was being taught in confirmation classes. (I left the class on the purported basis that I would instead be spending more time at Church with my parents).

I did accompany one or other of them to church occasionally – usually to Evensong, though sometimes Matins. The vicar for most of our time at Rodborough was the Reverend Rogers: a mild-mannered and rather nervous-looking man, who called at our house sometimes on pastoral visits. I am sure it was nothing to do with him, or indeed with my Sunday School experiences, but I did at one point become neurotic about religion – to the extent that I would make myself repeat the words of the Lord's Prayer over and over again. Fortunately, I mentioned this to my mother, who was able to persuade me that it was totally unnecessary, and, in fact, that it was a mental problem from which she herself had once suffered. I learned later that prior to getting married she had had herself to attend confirmation classes. This in turn had led to an obsession with religion, which took a more malignant form when she became afraid to hear mention of God's name. Maybe this was in the wake of the miscarriage I know she suffered before I was born. Whatever the cause, and having long returned to her normal extremely rational frame of mind, she was determined I would not be following a similar track.

Behind the Endowed School and next to the Church was a large cemetery, which stretched around the hillside towards Spillmans. It was between that and Walkley Hill that the Rectory Gardens were to be found. These had a gravelled exit on to Walkley Hill, which was about half-way between the Pike and the Church. The gardens possessed two large lawns at slightly different levels, surrounded by trees and bushes: quite a haven for all sorts of games and races, but now sadly disfigured with a formal play area.

At the lower end was an area immediately adjacent to the graveyard which was covered with shrubbery. In the midst of this Roger and I once found a small clearing, ideal as our "den". We would go and hide there every so often, though from what menace we were unspecific. Unfortunately for us, after a few weeks the bigger boys who had in fact created the clearing discovered our intrusion and evicted us once and for all.

The Rectory Gardens were also the venue for the annual church fete, where stalls and hooplas, and the sale of cakes and other produce provided an afternoon's delight. I would like to say that I had an eye for a bargain on such occasions, but the only purchase I remember making, was when I spent much of my pocket money on a healthy-looking cactus for my mother, only to be persuaded by another boy to swap it for the puny succulent he had bought for his.

The Rectory Gardens were an occasional pleasure. It was, however, far more likely, if my mother allowed us out, that, having exited Rock Cottages, we would turn not down Rodborough Hill, but up. In the first place, just beyond Mrs Cook's cottage at No 1 was a large flowering meadow, which ran down the hillside towards Kingscourt and Lightpill. It was often grazed by cattle, but, when it was not, it afforded not only space for games, but a profusion of flowers and butterflies the like of which is now rare. I doubt it survived into the 1970s. Down the far side of the field was a row of elm trees, which, had we but known, were similarly doomed. Within ten years Dutch

Elm Disease had claimed them, and they were felled and never replaced. As I lay in bed at night, I would draw back the curtains and watch the lights of the occasional car appearing and disappearing behind the foliage of those trees, as it negotiated the twists and turns of the lane below the Common.

Between the fields and the Common itself there was also Tabernacle Lane at a lower level. If you followed this past a few cottages on your left, it became thickly wooded till you reached the Tabernacle Church (which I also attended a few times with my father). Nearly opposite the Tabernacle was a steep path with steps which went down through woods to the Wolf Cubs' Hut. Like so many of my contemporaries, I gave this a try, but in my case only for a few weeks. I was particularly unskilled at tying reef knots and hated the Halloween Party I attended there, which involved apple bobbing and other games with which I was totally unfamiliar and inept. What clinched my decision to leave was a threat from some of the older boys to throw me all the way down the steps as my "initiation"! Socialisation outside family and school was not going well!

It was just above and beyond the flowering meadow that Rodborough Common itself began, at first a thin triangle of grass, crossed by a couple of tracks, but broadening as you ascended further. The Common proper then swelled before you, comprising the entirety of the crown of Rodborough Hill between the road from Cirencester to the left and the lane to the right which wound round above Kingscourt, hugging the broad haunches of the hillside till it climbed more steeply up to The Bear Hotel on the far side of the Common.

The hillside immediately above our cottage and the hill's flanks were quite steep as they climbed to their dominant peculiarity – Rodborough Fort: not an ancient encampment, but a turreted Victorian folly, the curtilage of which was surrounded by a high Cotswold stone wall. Within that enclosure and especially to the left was a considerable number of mature trees and hedges. Behind the fort, but still within its boundary wall, was a large generally level area which came to be used in the early '60s as a site for caravans.

The fort rarely seemed to be occupied, but there was an exception in the mid-1950s, when refugee children fleeing the failed Hungarian Uprising were briefly housed there. I have a mental image of a column of children marching up Rodborough Hill past our cottage on their way to the fort, though whether I actually saw this, merely heard about it or imagined it, I do not know. It must have been late in the year, for soon afterwards it was Bonfire Night, and the story ran that, seeing all of the fireworks exploding in the sky, the Hungarian children had been terrified, thinking the Russians had arrived to take them back to their homeland. At least one of the children is buried in Rodborough Churchyard.

The fort was also the destination of the annual May Walk: a local custom, held on the first Sunday in May, when local people followed the Salvation Army band up the hill and Common to sing hymns at the summit. Those attending would pick large bunches of cowslips as they made their way up. (This was then entirely legal.) May Walking was something about which my mother was particularly enthusiastic, and I know I stirred myself out of bed on at least one occasion to accompany her.

Behind the fort the Common extended across a large plateau (the first part of which comprised the caravan camp within the fort's boundary wall). On the right it plunged down to the lane above Kingscourt, and in particular to an area known as Little London. At the far end of the plateau was another walled and wooded area, which included an estate of expensive private housing. Beyond that were the Bear Inn to the right and Winstone's Ice Cream Shop to the left. Winstones was always the ultimate goal of family walks on the Common. At the front of a small factory, steps led down to a sales counter where standard brands of lollipop could be bought, but at which the real prize of any purchase was Winstone's own ice cream in a cone or wafer.

The location of the ice cream shop, of the private housing estate, and indeed of a derelict (but later restored) house which was situated in splendid isolation right on the front slope of the Common overlooking our cottage, must all have dated to an era before strict planning control, but it never occurred to us that they shouldn't be where they were. We simply accepted them as part of our environment and enjoyed them for themselves. The private roads on the housing estate were in fact delightful to walk along, what with the attractive post-war mansions and their many trees and hedges. My mother even took us blackberrying along the roads there one September morning before school.

More in keeping with the nature of the Common was the ancient cowshed to the left as you climbed the front of the hill, very close to the Cirencester Road. In our day that road marked a boundary between the generally open Common itself and a wooded area (known to us, due to the use often made of it, as "the Beanstick Wood"), where there was a rookery. In the decades after we left Rodborough trees invaded more and more of the Common at this point and the cowshed gradually vanished from sight, till the National Trust decided that the Common was beginning to lose its essential character, and quite a lot of clearing took place. In our time, up on the plateau there used to be a single tree, which my mother remembered from her childhood and which she called "The Lonely Tree". It has only very recently crashed to the ground.

Though we would walk as far as Winstone's with our parents, when expeditions on to the Common were mounted by Roger, Brenda, myself, and later my sister, we were bound by my mother's injunction always to remain in view from Rock Cottages, which meant that we could go right up as far as the fort, but that access to the sides of the Common and the area beyond was prohibited. Sometimes we would amuse ourselves by running down the steep slopes, kicking discuses of dried cow muck through the air as we went. More often we would confine ourselves to the old quarry area, which was on the right of the Common alongside the old drover's track which must have been the most direct route from Rodborough Village to Amberley in the past. The quarry was circular and mostly grassed over, but a fall of rubble had created a slippery slope from the top of the quarry to the bottom, and this provided a sort of ski slope down which you could slide, either standing or on your haunches. Such pastimes could fill an afternoon! Just above the quarry was a mound which, though small, was a prominent feature. This we called "The Mountain", in which Roger and I were convinced treasure was buried and at which periodically we dug and scraped to find the secret passages in which it would be concealed.

The mound must in fact have been no more than a spoil tip from the quarry itself!

The quarry was by no means alone as an example of past activities on the Common. At many points there were deep depressions where clearly Cotswold stone had been extracted, some of them quite extensive. In fact, quite an industry must have thrived at one time. None of these areas was active any more, and Nature had begun recolonising them all. Their original purpose was far more obvious then than it is now, when virtually all the old delvings have been reclaimed by the Common's usual long grasses and wildflowers. Though these were features I could only explore when my parents were with me, two large workings, apart from what we regarded as our own quarry, stick out in my memory. At the top of the Common on the right, again by the drover's track, was a very deep depression with fairly steep sides. If you could scramble down there, you would find that the bottom was very flat – maybe the edge of a particular stratum of rock or maybe even grassed-over hardstanding – and this was ideal for a cricket match – or an attempted one, for I was always hopeless at throwing and catching balls – as, I have to say, was my father! On the other side of the Common, between the fort and the road to Cirencester, was an even more extensive set of workings, which I visited much less frequently, though once when I went there with my father I found a fossil which, after consulting my child's encyclopaedia, I decided was a trilobite.

In 1961 or 1962 Stroud's first supermarket, Burton's, opened with considerable publicity, involving ribbon cutting, a minor celebrity, and the presence for a few days of several mascot chimpanzees! One evening Roger told me he'd heard that the chimpanzees had been taken for exercise on that part of the Common just beyond the trilobite quarry and behind the Beanstick Wood. The two of us set off, hopeful of seeing this wonder for ourselves. Unfortunately, as we approached the site, though we could see two chimpanzees being let out of a van, we found ourselves being shooed away by a keeper, who said there could not possibly be any more public viewings. The chimpanzees needed space! Unfortunately also, when we returned home, we were scolded by my mother for having broken her embargo against disappearing from view! Then and on later occasions, my mother would describe herself as having been "frantic", if ever she did not know where I or my sister were.

The Common, of course, was renowned for its magnificent views along the various Stroud Valleys reaching up to Painswick, out into the Severn Valley, and beyond as far as the Sugar Loaf near Abergavenny. Closer to home, you could look down upon the sprawling ugliness of Erinoid's factory in the Nailsworth Valley near Dudbridge. This was a major provider of employment in the area, though I don't think we knew anyone who actually worked there. (Ernie Gardiner was retired, Tom Heaven worked over at the Wagon Works in Gloucester, and Jean had her bread round.) From the top of the Common increasingly you could hear ice cream van chimes wafting up from the new estates at Lightpill, just below Kingscourt.

More memorable was the sound of skylarks – ever present in Spring and Summer - because wherever you walked you would be near their nests and they would need to distract you. As for wildlife more generally, I never saw a fox or a badger, or even a rodent on the Common, but butterflies, moths and insects were there in profusion. Catching grasshoppers or even cinnabar moths in a jam jar was a cruel, but popular pastime both at infant and junior schools. Of wildflowers, there were many types, but the most noteworthy were the bee orchids: extraordinary little mauve flowers with a large lip looking just like a bee extracting nectar. These grew in very few places. I once saw a jar of them in water on the top of Mrs Gardiner's kitchen cupboard. When I told Miss Bowering at the infant school (why did I decide this was necessary?), she was horrified. A bee orchid produced only one flower a year, and once that was picked it would not regenerate for twelve months.

As for animals of a more domesticated variety, there were some dogs, which walkers brought with them, but I do not remember dogs running free as they did in more urban areas. Then, of course, there were the cows, which grazed all over the Common, availing themselves of an inexhaustible supply of grass, but also of several cattle troughs. (Several years later a boy was killed when, tobogganing in the snow, he crashed into one of the troughs concealed by a drift.) For the most part, you could avoid the cows, if you wanted to. We did, however, once incorporate a herd of them into a game, where they were the Germans and we were the Allies.

I never felt threatened or in danger on the Common. No strange men ever spoke to me or attempted to abduct me, notwithstanding my mother's oft repeated warnings that there were such people about. There was, however, one strange woman who could be encountered on the Common, but who was more a figure of fun than someone to be feared. She was middle-aged and looked quite normal and respectable, but she brought all of her washing with her on to the Common and used to hang it out to dry on various hawthorn bushes, whilst playing with a ping-pong ball. One day on my way to school I saw her emerging with her washing basket from the canal towpath, from which I deduced, rightly or wrongly, that she first washed her clothes in the canal before climbing Rodborough Hill to dry them out. My mother admitted to me one day that this lady was related to us on her father's side, though I never ascertained quite how, or indeed what she was called.

CHAPTER 6

My father did not own a car. That isn't to say that he could not drive, for he had learnt after a fashion in the army, but whilst we lived at Rodborough almost all journeys were on foot or by bus.

The local bus service (the 429) ran from Queen's Road, just below the Pike, down Rodborough Hill and along the Bath Road into the centre of Stroud – originally to a stop outside the Post Office in Russell Street, but later calling instead at the new Stroud bus station in Merrywalks – and thence on to Brimscombe. Over the period of our lives at Rodborough the design of the buses changed from one with a slatted radiator cover rather like an elephant's upper trunk, to one with rounded, jolly, almost anthropomorphic features ("the Bristol L type"), and then to a square more modernistic front aspect. I must have used that bus so many times, though I have few specific memories of it. I do recall the pleasant savour of the chromium bars along the top of the seats, since I was addicted to sucking them, despite my mother's best efforts to stop me "catching something". I also remember very early on (or was reminded by my parents) that I had been scandalised to see on the seat in front of us a woman with a very lowcut back to her dress.

"Dat lady got no c'ose on," I announced to my mother, and to the rest of the bus.

As for the railway, this was used only when we went to Gloucester on the "Rail Car" or when we travelled to visit my father's sister and brother-in-law in far-away Norfolk. As a small child, I was scared of trains, or in particular the great emissions of steam which came from the engines, even what stationary at a platform. Once persuaded to enter a carriage, I would calm down, but would remain apprehensive that one of the "motes" from the engine, which my mother had warned me about, would enter any opened window and would lodge in my eye.

Most of our outings were, however, on foot: walks across the Common, or along the lanes which skirted it or went down into Kingscourt, or along Butterow Lane eastward from the Pike. Most often my sister and I went with our parents along the lanes to the right

49

of the Common. Sometimes this would take us up to The Bear Inn and back across the top. At other times we would turn down into Kingscourt and return by way of Walkley Hill. The lanes themselves were very narrow, deeply rustic and only lightly trafficked – as a few of them still are today. One respect in which they have improved over the years relates to the way the verges and hedgerows were managed. Back then, the verges were not mowed as they are today, but instead local authority workers sprayed weedkiller everywhere, leaving blackened and acrid-smelling foliage, which took weeks to recover.

We might also go walking along the lanes to the left of the Common mainly from our Pike to the Butterow Pike and then up to Winstones, or (by a much shorter route) from Butterow Lane by a side road up to the Beanstick Wood and back down Rodborough Hill.

There were access points from Butterow Lane, but also from King's Road (near my infant school) to the area known as Rodborough Fields, much beloved by Miss Bowering as an appropriate place for school nature walks, but developed for housing in the 60s. In the midst of the fields there was for some reason a tall iron rail structure, through which a spring fed waters which in turn nurtured watercress. When one year at school we watched frogspawn turn into tadpoles and then into frogs, this was where we released the baby frogs back into the wild.

If you walked down through the fields to the valley bottom you reached the railway viaducts over the Stroudwater Canal and River Frome. This was an eerie place, made more so by the story that my dad's dad, old Wilfy, had seen a ghost there! It was one of the routes you could take to Bowbridge and thence to my grandparents' house. It was also somewhere my father once took me when he went painting, with his oils and home-made easel. I still have the neo-Impressionist willows which resulted.

Sunday afternoons were when we most often went walking. Occasionally our parents would combine a walk with a bus ride, when they took us further afield to villages such as Bisley, Cranham, Nether Lypiatt (where the Manor – later the home of royalty – was also reputed to have a ghost) or Nailsworth. We might return part of the way on foot, part by bus.

When my sister was very small, she had to be carried a lot of the time, if not in her pushchair or pram. I even remember myself demanding to be carried on one occasion, when I was maybe as much as five years old and had become weary of lane-walking. My father agreed with what I took to be very bad grace.

It was in fact my mother who was the passionate walker of the family. Having sacrificed much of her youth to the War Years, she and her best friend, my godmother (Joan Taylor), and later my father too, had spent every opportunity up until my birth to go youth hostelling, firstly in Warwickshire, then further afield to Wales, the Lake District and even Scotland. She had two fat black photo albums which recorded the various holidays they had had. Alongside her tales of the War itself, she would often describe their walking adventures, particularly in the Brecon Beacons, where the hostel at Heol Senni, presided over by Winnie and Pop Clarke, held huge emotional significance for her. It was an assumption, which I and my sister shared, that in due course, when we grew up, we would do the same. In the interim, going for a good long walk by way of training, however tiring, was a means to an inevitable end.

My Uncle Maurice did have a car and usually took all four of us out for a big trip whenever he had been staying with us – as a "thank you". There were trips at other times of the year too. Because of the distances involved, and the poor quality of roads and cars alike at the time, these journeys would be to places such as Weston-super-Mare and Bristol Zoo, small resorts on the South Wales coast, like Llantwit Major, Barry Island and Porthcawl, but occasionally as far as Weymouth on the South Coast. The abysmal sea-side food, the fact that my sister and I would often suffer from carsickness (usually because my mother had decided that orange juice was the best thing for a child's stomach on a journey), and the way Maurice's car frequently broke down in no way undermined the importance we attached to such departures from the Stroud Valleys. These were our grand adventures.

On one occasion, when I was very young and Maurice's car ground to its usual halt, I am said to have announced: "Uncle Mar's car no good!"

On another, when in fact I was taken out by Maurice, not with my immediate family, but with my grandparents, I remember him scrambling down a bank to a little stream to fetch water for his leaking car radiator in the little bucket I had brought with me for making sandcastles. The weather was so awful that day that it was the only use to which the bucket was put. Though I very much enjoyed trips out with Uncle Maurice, I was always a grumbler on such occasions. Maurice never took offence, but would simply look at me curiously and say in measured tones: "What a funny boy!"

Apart from Summer Holidays, trips out with Maurice, the occasional day trip by coach to Weston or Bristol Zoo, and a couple of weekend trips we made to stay with my father's army friend, John Packford, and his family in Oxford, the main events in our lives – the highlights and prime sources of enjoyment – revolved entirely around interactions with our wider family.

The relatives we saw most were my grandparents on my maternal side. (My father's parents had both died before I was born.) They were Mort and Florrie Teal; he: thick-set, balding, with a rather large chin, and increasingly deaf; she: small, thin with very fine grey/ white hair tied up in a bun and always covered, when she went out, by a hat secured with a large pin. They lived at 17 Lower Lypiatt Terrace, Horns Road, at the far end of that road from Holy Trinity Church, close to the children's playground known as the Daisy Bank. They had lived there at least since the late 1920s, when the houses in the terrace were offered by Holloways, the clothing factory, to employees, such as my grandfather, first on a tenancy and then for purchase freehold. They would remain there until firstly my grandfather died and then a few years later, my grandmother went into a home towards the end of the 1970s.

The house was in a very long terrace and was tiny, though my mother maintained it was a palace compared with the slum dwelling the family had previously inhabited in Chapel Street. The front door was never locked in daytime and had neither bell nor knocker. You simply pushed it open and shouted "Coo-ee" to attract attention. A narrow passage led from the front door to the stairs, with two doors on the left: one to the front room, which was kept for best and in consequence hardly ever used, and the other to the back room, which served as sitting room, dining room, and anything else appropriate. In the back room was a utility-ware extending table, several utility-ware straight backed chairs, a couple of easy chairs, a sideboard, and (later) a radiogram. There was also an old-fashioned grate, with a metal rack which could be lowered over the flames and on which Gran boiled her old black kettle. Alongside, but still within the grate, were metal cupboards, in which presumably you could have kept food warm, though for the most part they were used to store kindling wood.

From the back room you went up a step to the cold rather dark kitchen with its laundry boiler, gas cooker and a basin with cold tap. There was a bowl in the basin, which contained dirty water in which you washed your hands when you had been to the toilet or done some gardening. The water was changed probably only once or twice a day, because, though there was running water, it was ingrained with my grandparents that water was precious!

Once or twice I also encountered in the kitchen a large bucket standing on the floor and all of a writhe and a churn with elvers. These were a seasonal delicacy brought up to Stroud from the Severn and purchased for a shilling a bucket. (Nowadays a bucketful would be worth many hundreds (thousands?) of pounds, and its contents would never find their way on to a local breakfast table, for they are all exported to Spain, the Middle East and Japan!) I never ate them myself, and was rather revolted by my grandfather's relish as he described how you dropped them live into hot fat, from which they would jump with their eyes popping out!

Most cooking was, of course, done by my grandmother, who produced thick, glutinous meat stews, garnished with rock-hard dumplings; similarly rock-hard fried steak, served with delicious blackened chips cooked in lard; and meat rissoles, the recipe for which my grandmother could never explain, since she didn't work by way of measured ingredients, but merely by their feel! My grandfather also cooked on occasions and did so rather well, but nobody was supposed to know this, because it was "women's work".

From the living room, you could also access a little pantry under the stairs. Someone had hanged themselves inside the pantry in the days when the property had been used as a pub, though how anyone would have had room to stage an effective suicide in that tiny space was a mystery. It is strange, but we never had any fear that there was a resultant ghost – such would have been too inconvenient for daily living and was a luxury only to be associated with the railway viaducts and Nether Lypiatt Manor!

On the first floor there were just two bedrooms and a boxroom. The box room was for many years occupied by Maurice as his bedroom, but became a small bathroom in the late '60s. The second bedroom had been my mother's and then was taken over by Maurice after her marriage. The front bedroom was my grandparents'. It was, in fact, in this room, after my grandfather's death, that my grandmother convinced herself that she was being visited by **his** ghost, her terror at which resulted in her being removed to a care home.

Out the back of the house was a small paved yard with a water butt, which had an acrid stagnant smell, and a drain which had the more pleasant odour of old tea leaves, alongside which grew Lilies-of-the-Valley. At the further end of the yard was the outside (and only) toilet (in which the paper was Izal, rather than Bronco, but there wasn't much to choose between them!), and beside it a large coal shed. Steps then led up to the garden, which sloped steeply to Summer Street. If you went a little way up the garden and looked back, you were faced at the lowest level by a corrugated iron roof, which covered the coal shed and privy. On the brick wall above this there was an old metal sign bearing an advertisement – again dating back to the property's previous incarnation as a pub.

My grandmother had a succession of cats: Kitch and Blackie during my time. For them my grandmother would boil fish and put it just inside the coal shed. Every so often this would attract rats, which my grandfather had to deal with. One Sunday we came visiting and found the place permeated by a hideous smell. It seemed that a rat had somehow entered the house, had gone under the floorboards of the sitting room and had died there. We did not enjoy our tea that day! Later in the week, when the stench became unbearable, my grandfather, assisted by Maurice, managed to clear the furniture and raise a couple of floorboards, though not the boards immediately over the rat's carcass. He reached along and grabbed at the corpse, only to have the whole skin come away in his hand! It was another story he told with relish. He had a burial ground for rats right at the top of the garden. It was an area I avoided.

My grandfather was still working in the 1950s and early 60s, having been born in 1891. We therefore saw less of him than my grandmother, though he would always be there, if we visited on a weekday evening or at the weekend. He was a man of considerable intelligence, but very little education, having been kept home from school by his mother to help her with the piecework she received from one of the mills. He had very definite ideas about things, including politics. He was a Working Class Tory and maintained that whenever the Labour Party was in power it always put tax on those things which were important to the working man, namely beer and fags. He took strong dislikes to individuals in the public eye. Jean Metcalfe, who hosted the BBC's "Two Way Family Favourites", was a particular target. He could not understand how she could be paid for what she did, whereas, his friend, Bill Lampard down in the town, "would be glad to do it" for free! Later on, George Best became his bête noir. He would launch into an attack as soon as we entered the living room:

"What d'ya think of Georgie Best, then?" This would not be followed by a critique of the player's skill as a footballer, but rather by: "'ee d' make easel' look so silly with that beard" (and Gramp would then use his hands to mimic a whispy beard under his own chin. "'ee be like 'ee wot burnt the cakes!" was his clinching insult.

Gramp loved funny stories (or at least stories he thought were funny), amusing routines, and novelties such as you could buy in seaside kiosks and joke shops. During the War, he had trained one of the family's cats (Goofus) to do a Nazi salute when he said "Heil, Hitler!" By Blackie's time, the same trick had been changed to the more peaceable: "How d'ya do? How d'ya do? How d'ya do? Shake a paw!" and Blackie would dutifully raise his front leg for a formal greeting.

My grandfather also had a story, which he thought hilarious, though no one else did, which revolved about a confusion between a sack of potatoes and a sack of pig shit. It amused us more to learn that, when they were adolescents, he used to say to my mother and uncle: "Don't know why y' d' go to the pictures. You d' get more fun out of a fart!"

My grandfather's passion, though, was gardening, and he maintained a fair-sized vegetable patch at the house and a separate allotment off Bowbridge Lane until he was in his 80s. He loved growing flowers for his small front garden and for the borders round a small grassed area just above the coal shed and just below his rows of cabbages and potatoes. My mother used to say that he had kept the family well fed during World War II, and that rationing had been no great problem, especially since he and Maurice refused to eat butter, so that Florrie and my mum enjoyed double the normal allowance. The fertility of the garden and allotment before, during and after the War owed much, it was said, to the store's horse, whose droppings my grandmother would gather up on a shovel as soon as they were deposited in Horns Road, and then transport still steaming through the house and out to the back garden!

My grandparents' general conversation itself could be earthy, as could my mother's, though with her it could be a pose she sometimes adopted for effect, whereas with my grandparents it was simply the way they were. My grandmother, for instance, relished little rhymes, such as:

"Pea s'up, penny a quart,
That's the stuff to make y' fart".

And then there was a story she used to tell (too long to recite here), which concluded with the words:

"Yes, mam; no, mam; thank you, mam; please.
Up the duck's arse you'll find the green peas!"

Their descriptions of people were scatological in the extreme. A short person was only "a turd and a half high", and, if fat too, "built like the half side of a shithouse". Someone who attempted to improve their appearance looked "like a bag of shit done up ugly". Someone who looked sad or disappointed looked "shitten". Someone who was inquisitive "d' wanna know the ins and outs of a cat's arse"!

It was not only at Horns Road that we saw more of my grandmother than my grandfather, for she would also visit us on her own at Rodborough on Thursday afternoons, travelling by bus and always bringing sweets. She was a doting grandmother, though I formed little impression of her real personality till years later, for much was hidden with her. She enjoyed company, though she was shy and would never join in party games at Christmas. She loved to chat with her neighbours and various other friends, like Mrs Yates next-door and Mrs Seymour, who lived along the road and whose teeth were so prominent that it was joked that she wore two sets of false ones at the same time. Such socialising was frowned on, however, by Mort, who would be rude and unwelcoming, if anyone he didn't know or like called at the house. My mother told me that once Florrie had a particular friend, whom Mort referred to as "Fat Busky", and to whom he encouraged my mother and her brother as children to be so cheeky and unpleasant that in the end she stopped calling.

My memories of my grandmother at this time were simple: delight, as I sat on her knee by the fire in her tiny living room, having her explain to me about the neighbours, and the neighbours' rabbit, and the flowers in the garden, as we looked out of her window up the garden to Summer Street beyond; expectation, as her Thursday visit with its promise of sweets approached (an attitude for which my mother reproached me); hilarity, when, once on a visit to Rodborough, she took me and my sister (who was in a pram) along Butterow Lane, and managed to wheel it right into a huge pile of cow-muck, but then stood there just laughing at the absurdity of it all.

At home at Lower Lypiatt Terrace my grandmother spent a lot of time sitting by the fire – so close, that she frequently burned her shins! From time to time, she would yawn, but it was no ordinary yawn. Rather it mimicked the pitch and tune of her wall clock chime!

My grandmother, whose hearing was much better than her husband's, liked to listen to the wireless, and in the early 60's was well abreast of the pop charts. On a coach trip to Weston once I caught her singing

Brian Hyland's "Sealed with A Kiss". Early in 1964 she was very keen on a track by The Searchers, though her hearing was not that good, since she thought it was called "Needles and Fingers", rather than "Needles and Pins"! At the end of the previous year my grandfather's Christmas card to her had been a postcard of the Beatles, though his own taste tended more to novelty songs and in due course to Jim Reeves and the Seekers. (He was intolerant of classical music, and if he heard a soprano, was likely to say: "Oh, give her a carrot!")

We would most often visit my grandparents on a Sunday afternoon. In Summer we might walk all the way to Horns Road, but our journey back and visits at other times of the year used the bus service. Generally, we would while away the time there having tea, playing with "the bricks" (which were strips of wood which my grandfather had cut up and painted specifically for the amusement of his grandchildren), perhaps watching the tv, certainly listening to "Pick of the Pops", but generally the adults would just chat about neighbours, relations, gardening, the weather – and who had died recently. I used to love listening to them and would join in where I could. On one occasion, when marriage was being discussed, I announced that I would never marry, but was going to have lots of children!

My grandmother's usual refrain when we arrived would be: "An't we 'ad some weather!", which would apply whether it had been good, bad or indifferent. If the weather was in fact good, we might also go for a walk from Lower Lypiatt Terrace, though my grandparents themselves would never come unless it was along to the nearby cemetery. There was the Daisy Bank to visit with its swings and see-saws, but beyond that there were walks up the valley past a place known as the Wayhouse. It was an area said to be infested with adders, so it was not something I was keen on, though my mother was strangely blasée about it, her usual fears for our safety outweighed by a confidence instilled in her own childhood. If we went to the cemetery, it would be to look at or tend family graves. On one occasion, I found moon daisies growing in profusion and started to pick a bunch. For whatever reason, my father (abetted by my grandfather) then warned me against this, because they were nourished on dead bodies! At once I rushed back to my grandmother's and scrubbed my hands in the grey slimy water in the kitchen basin.

I felt very close to my grandmother, less so to my grandfather. That said, physical contact was at a minimum with them both, once I was too big to sit on my grandmother's knee. As with other relatives (with one exception,) affection was expressed, not by kisses and cuddles, but by bringing sweets when we were to meet, and giving a small amount of money when we parted. Years later, when I went to see my grandparents before leaving for university, I was quite nonplussed when my grandfather shook my hand (something he might have done with the cat, but never with me before), and my grandmother gave me a whiskery kiss.

They showed little outward affection for each other too. She referred to him as "our dad" or "our chap" and would often say: "Oh, 'ee! – 'ee d' give I gyp!", or "'Ee d' get I down".

If Mort called her anything, it was "'ooman".

When years later he died, her words as he was laid to rest were, however, a regretful, "No one to lean on, n'more."

There were other relatives of my grandparents whom we saw less frequently, if at all. My grandmother had relatives in America, plus her Cousin Beattie, who lived down towards Bowbridge. I never met any of the former until the 1980s, after my grandmother had died. Probably due to my grandfather, I never ever met Cousin Beattie!

Despite my grandfather's age, he himself still had two living aunts: one called Mabel, whom I only recall waving to from outside her gate on Middle Street. She died in the 1950s, but was survived for several years by her sister, Kate, who lived in what seemed a much more modern house not far from my grandparents. She would sit in the corner at Christmas parties, rather too old to participate, but enjoying the company. She had an obsession with keys and locks, but would often fail to find the right key for the right lock: a problem which it always fell to my grandfather to sort out.

Then there were my grandfather's sisters: Aunty Mue and Aunty Gert, both older than him. Aunty Mue lived at Woodbine Villas in Bath Road, on the stretch between Walkley Hill and the bottom of Rodborough Hill. Hers was a terraced house which was primitive, even by the standards of the 1950s. Apart from its reliance on an outside loo and an old-fashioned grate for warmth, it had no electricity at all. Lighting was still by way of gas lamps, which each evening had to be lowered from the ceiling and the wick ignited with a taper. As a tenant, her attitude was that she would not spend money improving the property for the benefit of her landlord, and clearly neither was he in the business of improving living conditions for his tenants.

Aunty Mue had poor sight, but would not visit an optician, so, in the evenings in particular, and in later years when she came to our house and watched tv, her eyes would water and tears would run down her cheeks. Neither would she visit a dentist, and so had no more than a very few teeth left (having removed the others by the age-old method of the slammed door and attached string). Those teeth she retained she would discourse upon and waggle with her fingers to show how loose even they had become. She had once had a fine head of hair, I was told, but it was now just a frizzy mass of uncombed white strands. I once watched as a spider span its web from one of those strands to her shoulder.

She had been a widow since the early 1950s. Her late husband, Percy Knight (a great drinker and the soul of a party, according to family legend), she always disparaged as "Knighty", or, according to my mother (but not within my hearing), "Knight-Shite". We would see Aunty Mue and her son, Lewis (very much in the mould of his father), at Christmas, but on probably no more than one other occasion in the year, unless we bumped into her by chance when shopping, and had to endure the waggling of her teeth.

Her younger sister, Gert, was a very different personality. Whereas Mue could be earthy and aggressive, Gert was a spinster, had a low opinion of men and their intentions, and attended the parish church every Sunday. Her moral rigour was illustrated on one occasion when a workman was admitted to her house to do some repairs. True or not, Aunty Gert maintained that in the course of his work he had touched her leg. (She was most certainly in her 70s at the time). "GET OUT," she bawled, pointing to the front door with the gesture of an Old Testament prophet, and this he did, never to return – or to be paid for whatever works he had already done!

Gert loved to talk… and talk, and talk. And once conducted, a conversation with one individual would often be recycled and repeated as part of her conversation with the next: "She turned round and said….'ee turned round and said"…"I turned round and said"…punctuating the recitation, as appropriate. So much so, that Maurice once commented that she and her collocutors must have been spinning like tops! Once the revolutions had ceased, and agreement had been reached, she would often say in triumph: "Yer! You be just like I!"

She also adhered to wise saws and superstitions, such as "Wear green, and th' 'll soon wear black," and "Never put new shoes on the table"!

Later on, she was convinced that I was cultivating a kiss curl, since in her day that had been a way of attracting the opposite sex – in her case, without much success. In fact, it was just the way my hair grew of its own accord.

Into the 60s Gertie still worked - again at Holloways, the clothes manufacturer – and maybe in consequence it was considered that her laundry should be done for her by Aunty Mue, who had not worked since her marriage. For that and no doubt for a host of other reasons, they used to fight like cats, particularly at Christmas parties. Gert was fairly phlegmatic and never gave way. Mue was excitable and would end up shaking with rage.

Gert lived in Middle Street until 1963 in a house which was almost as decrepit as Mue's. It did have electricity, but its staircase was dangerous, having been left to rot away in places. We never went to Aunty Gert's for tea, and I remember being in her house only once. She did come to us a few times, though, and was game enough to go for a walk with my mother and myself and sister on the Common – something I never recall Mue undertaking.

In fact, Mue only walked from her house into Stroud and back to shop at Woolworths. She had a shopping basket with wheels. "'ee d' run away with I," she'd say, describing her walk home down from Rowcroft.

 Once when we were visiting Woolworths with my Gran, she espied a figure moseying along another aisle. "It be Aunty Mue," she wailed. "We bent a gonna talk to 'er!'", so we hid and, as soon as we could, scuttled from the store.

CHAPTER 7

There was a difference in social class between my mother's and my father's families. My mother's family was working class, whereas my father's was lower middle to middle, and thought itself even better! My great-grandfather, John White, had arrived in Stroud from Cornwall in the 1860s/70s and had established a printing firm, which was taken over by his son, Arthur Wilfrid (known as "Wilf"), on John's death in 1917. They were therefore small businessmen and from the beginning of the new century also owned what must then have been quite a desirable residence at 25 Lansdown, near the centre of Stroud. (Previous to taking over both that house and the business, Wilf had lived with his young family at Rodborough!)

John married Mary Watson from Lincolnshire; and Wilf's wife, Mabel, was his cousin from the same stock. Wilf and his mother were both fascinated by family history, and Wilf, in fact, compiled a maternal family tree, which my father possessed and over which we pored every so often. The point of greatest pride at the head of the tree was the name of one Lewis Watson, Baron Rockingham, who lived during the first half of the seventeenth century and fought on the Royalist side. For her part, Mary had penned an article which appeared in the local press (early in the 1900s) under the title "The Family Name of Watson". This referred to all sorts of lords and ladies mainly from the early modern period, which, it was implied, all belonged to the same family, and, as if to add additional caché, there was the sentence: "I do myself possess a collection of Queen Anne spoons".

In later years, when I delved into family history, I discovered that there was, in fact, no connection at all between Baron Rockingham and anyone in our family. He - together with an alleged Admiral Watson, friend of Clive of India - had simply been attached to the top section of the Watson tree, which otherwise comprised mainly skilled craftsmen from Lincolnshire and the East Riding of Yorkshire. Furthermore, when with the eye of an adult I came to read Mary's article more carefully, I realised that, despite the heading, there was again no evidence of any connection to the personages mentioned. In fact, it was no more than a mere impression that, because Mary shared the same surname, she must be their descendant! The Watson noble

63

heritage was fiction, and as for the Whites, John White's own father died in the Penzance workhouse.

There were other snippets I picked up concerning Mary White (Née Watson) – two of them consistent with the picture of someone who was status-obsessed. In the first place, she was said in the family to have been one of the first women to attend Cambridge University, even if she was unable to take a degree. I have no idea whether this was true of not. It seems highly unlikely. Secondly, she loathed "Radicals and Chapelonians". Finally, though, and more endearingly, she was reputed often to walk from Lansdown to Ebley and back, which took her past Stroud Brewery where she would stop and inhale deeply. Her partiality and that of her husband for a tipple was another family story, but less trumpeted!

Two generations down – my father and his sisters – made no great play of the alleged family history, but there was an unspoken assumption that the family had come from better things; hence my father's liking for the description "faded gentility". My mother would adopt the same expression with regard to the Whites, though had no such delusions about her own family. In fact, she rather rejoiced in being, like them, "grosse et grasse" and "of the earth, earthy"!

The combination of the snobbery of the Whites and the contrarian attitudes of my mother's family (in particular of my grandfather) led my parents to be rather sneering with regard to other people – though often behind their backs. The Working Classes and Trade Union bosses were easy targets, as were all Labour politicians. Popular culture was also something which they looked down on. It was the era when girls' skirts were becoming shorter and shorter, and frequently when one or more girls passed us in the street, or when we were on one of our Sunday walks, my parents would look at each other in complicit disgust and, once out of earshot, would complain about the fatness or hideousness of the legs displayed. Maybe this was also a result of sexual inhibitions, but whatever the cause, it became learned behaviour for me. Some years later in a school art lesson the master asked us what we thought of the miniskirt. At once I came out with the White party-line on the unsightliness of it all, only to be surprised that the master and the rest of the class were of another view. It took me quite a while to realise that sometimes the pooled wisdom of the Whites and Teals was far from conventional – or even correct.

Another difference between my mother's and father's families was that we saw much less of his relatives, since, except for his middle sister, Alice, they no longer dwelt in Gloucestershire. My father's oldest sister, Dorothy (sixteen years his senior) lived in Norfolk with her husband, Brian Bowle. They were, therefore, people we visited for Summer holidays (three times whilst we lived at Rodborough), but whom otherwise we would see only briefly, usually twice a year, when they visited Brian's mother and sisters, who lived at Amberley. Dorothy and Brian were a very different prospect to any of my mother's relatives. He was a tall pipe-smoking deputy-headmaster, who had indeed been to Cambridge. She was diminutive, and before her marriage had played piano for the silent movies at the local cinema. They were Quakers, were fairly left-wing in their views (though before her marriage Dorothy had been an Empire Loyalist!), were extremely cultured – and, in particular, obsessed with classical music (as long as it wasn't Wagner, whom they abhorred, or Tchaikovsky, who was merely "tuneful".) They were both, however, very kind and jovial, if a little intense, and Dorothy in particular idolised children, "young people" and their potential.

It was clear that my mother was slightly cowed by them, and she often impressed on us the need to behave when they came to visit. Unfortunately, on one occasion either she had forgotten to remind us of this, or I simply became confused as to which relatives needed to be impressed with good behaviour and which not. Against that fateful backdrop, we went for a walk with them on the Common.

"There's a turd behind that hedge," I crowed at one point.

"I bowed off," announced my sister, once we had returned with them to 4 Rock Cottages and she and I were sliding with raucous delight down the backs of the furniture.

My mother retired in despair to the kitchen, but (as she later told me) Dorothy followed her: "Children can be so embarrassing, can't they?" she consoled with a smile, to my mother's infinite gratitude.

Brian and Dorothy had a daughter, my cousin Jane, whom we saw very rarely at this time, since she was 15 years older than me and very much undergoing education. I recall her being at Swaffham when we holidayed there in 1956, and on that occasion she came with us on a trip to Hunstanton, where I told her that the reason she couldn't see the starfish that I had just discovered was that I had "littler eyes" than she did! I also recall a brief visit to Rodborough when she came to introduce her fiancé, Clive, in 1960, and took Ros and myself for a walk on the Common. However, neither Ros nor I, nor indeed our mother attended her wedding later that year, presumably to avoid the travel expense of going to Reading, where both Jane and Clive had been at university.

Brian, Dorothy and Jane (at least in her youth) were no more physically demonstrative than my mother's family. The conventional greeting was a handshake. "My, how you've grown," Dorothy would say, as she seized our hands; whilst on departure Brian might well beam at us and leave us half a crown each. Once, when Brian himself shook my hand, I immediately experienced a sharp pain in the palm, and on looking down saw blood! When I muttered about this to my father, he explained that years before Brian had damaged his hand on a broken wash basin, and ever since had had a crooked finger. This, he guessed, had caused my injury!

My father's youngest sister, Nancy, lived in London (where she had gone to work in the Civil Service during the Blitz – another example of an overwhelming desire to escape!) In the early 50s she had married one Joe Lampitt, and they had gone to live in Uxbridge and then Hillingdon, whilst both continuing to work in London. We met up with Nancy when we had to change stations and trains in London on our way to Norfolk in 1956. I have an impression on that occasion of a tall and elegant lady in elegant clothes, but that was my 3-year-old perspective. She was, in fact, fairly short (as were my parents) and rather broad in the beam, but she did have the White Family's jet-black hair and did indeed wear clothes of quality. There was a slight resemblance to Eartha Kitt.

Like Dorothy and Brian, she and Joe would visit the West Country once or twice a year to see her family in Stroud, but also his relatives in

Malvern. Once Joe called on his own for some reason, whilst only my mother, sister and myself were home. Maybe he had expected to see my father, who was at work, and was disappointed, so he didn't stay long, and I remember him becoming irritated with me when he'd asked me when the next bus was due, and I had been unable to tell him. My parents often found me annoying, it was true, but this was the first time that any other relative had spoken to me sharply for mere ignorance, and I did not like it.

Nancy also came to see us once on her own, and then stayed several days, taking the little bedroom up in the attic. I must have been ill at the time, for I remember her visiting me repeatedly in my bedroom, where we would play on the bed with my model prehistoric animals. She could keep me laughing like nobody else, for she was continually adopting comic voices and telling stories, and generally behaving much more like a child than an adult. When it was time for her to go back to London, I remember being shocked that she did something else adults never did: she burst into tears, so sorry was she to be leaving us.

Nancy spoke rapidly and very quietly - almost in a whisper. She would speak on the intake of breath as well, almost as if she was fearful time would run out for what she wanted to say. She was so apologetic too – everything she did needed to be excused, though often with a strong element of self-deprecation at the scrapes she'd managed to get herself into. Once Brian observed that he and Dorothy had met Nancy at a London station "apologising for her very existence"!

Later I was to discover from my parents that in the early '50s Nancy had suffered a nervous breakdown – something to do, my mother speculated, with her relationship with Joe before they were married. It had resulted in her going home from London to Lansdown, where, rather than her condition recovering, it became worse. My father said that one evening that week they had had to hide the knives and that Nancy had been obsessing about shaming "the family escutcheon", whatever that was: perhaps another invention of old Wilf. Eventually, she was committed to the local mental hospital at Coney Hill on the outskirts of Gloucester, where my parents found her in a padded cell. She was released some months later, and was helped to recuperate by my mother who took her away to Devon for a holiday. (It had never occurred to me, until this explanation of Nancy's mental health emerged, to question why one of the family photograph albums showed pictures of a solitary holiday involving my mother and Nancy, and yet no one else.)

The reason why Nancy spoke so quietly, was so lacking in confidence, and had left Stroud for London in 1940 was almost certainly down to my father's third and middle sister, Alice. Ten years older than my father, and twelve years older than Nancy, she must have been a dominating and perhaps intimidating character in the White Family household, especially after Dorothy had married in the late '20s, and even more so after the death of their mother from cancer in 1938, when both my father and Nancy were still in their teens.

Alice was in many ways an extremely unfortunate person, born with a cleft palate and hare lip. This made her extremely self-conscious, and in photographs she often tilted her head away from the direction of the camera to conceal her disfigurement. At my mother's suggestion in the early 50s, she had had the operation to graft over the split in her lip – an operation then in its infancy - and this had left her with a large red and raw-looking area of skin beneath her nose. This must have been desensitised, since, especially when she ate, candlesticks of mucous would often descend to her mouth. (It was usually my mother who had to point this out.) The operation also failed to remedy her very indistinct speech. The combination of her inability to pronounce certain consonants and a rather harsh-sounding voice, hardened further by constant smoking, made it difficult to understand what she said. Her response to blank stares and incomprehension was to become angry and to repeat anything which had not been understood more loudly (but no more clearly) than before.

Alice was also blind in one eye, had poor vision in the other, and suffered with her joints and with varicose veins. She visited quite frequently, rather to the annoyance of my mother with whom she often argued, and when she visited it was always part of the proceedings for her to refer to her varicose veins, and then to peel off layers of stockings and bandages to reveal her legs for universal inspection. They resembled Danish Blue cheese, according to my father. My mother's oft stated and disapproving view was that Alice's many misfortunes were entirely due to the fact that her parents had been first cousins.

When she had been at school Alice had suffered bullying and ridicule and so had learned to defend herself physically, becoming known as "Boxer White". At some stage she must also have rebelled against her own family by deciding to "talk proper Stroud", unlike the rest of the Whites, who all spoke grammatically, but with a slight bur. Whenever she arrived at our house her greeting was always a gruff: "'ow be ya?"

Strange to say that, despite her verbal difficulties and her adopted way of speaking, she was a very literate writer of letters – frequently to the local paper about politics, concerning which she had strong, but mutable views. She was similarly talented when it came to drawing and draughtsmanship and in the 50s was employed at Hill Paul (near the railway station), where those skills were utilised. In later life she became quite prolific with her oil portraits mainly of people in the public eye, which she based on small photographs reproduced in the "Radio Times", but she would often use no more than odd scraps of paper on which to work, and so her pictures would curl up and disintegrate and were never shown to anyone outside the family.

If a visit from Alice was an event which to a small boy was enjoyable, but tinged with a sense of danger, the occasional visit to Alice's own house was daunting for other reasons. She still lived during the '50s and early' 60s in what had been the White Family's house since the turn of the century: 25 Lansdown. Whereas my parents had lived on the top floor before we had moved to Rodborough, and other rooms, including the basement, had been let out, Alice's lair was on the ground floor. There she had a front room complete with dining table and chairs, piano, sideboard, and tv; a kitchen (which was utterly filthy); and a bedroom in which a large bed was piled high with blankets, since she felt the cold. There was a small wc halfway up the staircase to the first floor. The whole apartment reeked of cigarette smoke and cat pee, for, despising much of the human race, Alice had a succession of feline companions, who were never properly trained. In the '50s it was Tiger who was in residence. Later came Felix (or "Fe-yal", as she called him), and then Tom. It was clear my mother took a dim view of the smell, its origins, and the general lack of hygiene. She would eye the cutlery and whatever Alice served up for tea with deepest suspicion.

On the one hand, I was fond of Aunty Alice, always finding her entertaining in a bizarre sort of way, and in fact never realising how off-putting her appearance and behaviour could be to others, since it was what I had known since my earliest years when we had lived in the same building. I was even inured to the slobbery kisses she used to bestow on myself and Ros whenever she visited – always accompanied by a vocalised "mmmmmmm!" On the other hand, and in retrospect, it was easy to see how life with Alice had driven both my father and Nancy to seek refuge away from Stroud. – in the army and the Blitz!

My father maintained that Alice had also had a stormy relationship with their father, Wilf, who had died in 1951. Apparently, she kept hammering through "The Ride of the Valkyrie" on her out-of-tune piano, as the old man lay dying upstairs. More generally, before that final vignette, she would bully him, whilst he would make fun of her. A story ran that one afternoon Wilf went into one of the local cinemas and saw Alice sitting in there on her own. He crept up beside her and placed his hand on her knee.

"Get off me, you filthy bugger," she shouted and stormed off to a safer seat. (So much for gentility – faded or otherwise!) It's debateable quite what molestation she feared, because I later learned that Alice had little knowledge of the Facts of Life until she was in her late 40s, when again it fell to my mother to enlighten her, after a Lithuanian refugee (who spoke no English), started to take an unwonted interest in Alice – or perhaps in what he assumed might be her family wealth.

"Bugger" seemed to be one of her favourite words. She used to refer to her stiff knee as "this bugger", and years later I remember her dismissing Edward Kennedy as "that rubbishy bugger"!

Her life was not one of continual aggression and hostility, however. She liked a party, especially if it involved whisky, and she liked her food, though it would be more correct to say she liked eating. If she came to us for tea, she would gorge herself on sausage rolls and ladle cream onto everything. "'en I awful," she would say, and cackle appreciatively.

But she was no cook herself. When my father returned home after World War II, after 7 years of army rations, she served for him her special hot pot, which she would heat and reheat for several days, and of which the only identifiable ingredient was cabbage. My father, despite all his years of deprivation and undoubted feelings of family loyalty, could not bring himself to eat it. I can only imagine her expression.

CHAPTER 8

During each of the first 10 years of my life (most of which were spent at Rodborough), we usually had a Summer holiday. The years when we did not were 1953 (when I was born), 1957 (when my sister was born), and 1959 (when I don't think my parents could afford a holiday and ironically there was a beautiful warm Summer!)

My first holiday was to Weston-Super-Mare when I was 18 months old (and my father introduced me to the subject of myxomatosis!) Of the following year in Paignton, I remember even less, apart from the fact that we stayed in a bed and breakfast and that we visited Grace Burrows (a friend of my mother from the War Years) in her office at Marks & Spencer in Exeter. For the decade after that holiday, we always stayed either in a caravan or in Norfolk at the home of Dorothy and Brian. A Norfolk holiday would last as much as 10 days, since there were no costs for accommodation and few for food. Other holidays would be for no more than a week. Apart from financial considerations, the length of holidays also depended on the fact that my father's annual entitlement was never more than 2 weeks.

My uncle and aunt lived in Swaffham at 18 Market Place, which was one half of a large flint-covered, probably eighteenth-century house in the middle of the town, and was a perk of my uncle's role as Deputy Headmaster of Hamonds Grammar School. (The Headmaster and his family occupied the other half of the building.) It was much more spacious than our own home, even had out-houses, and also a large garden comprising not only a lawn, borders, and a wooded area, but also a large vegetable patch, on all of which my uncle lavished scrupulous care. Needless to say, the whole property seemed palatial to me, though when I visited it many years later as an adult, long after my uncle and aunt had left, I was amazed how small the front room (then used for small art exhibitions) in fact was.

As a child, I delighted in the novelty of sleepy Swaffham, with its Butter Market and other historic buildings, in which my aunt kindled my interest by giving me the relevant Eye-Spy book. I was also fascinated by the various places you could visit in the surrounding county, all by means of small diesel trains, which passed field after field bristling with pheasants, which my sister and I had never encountered in Gloucestershire, and which we would count to see which of us could spy out the greater number during our stay.

We first went to Swaffham as a family in 1956, then again in 1961 and 1963. At that point, the unstated implication that we should go to stay in Norfolk every other year from then on was stamped on by my mother. It was not that she did not enjoy the company and being waited on, but in those days, when we had no car, what we saw of Norfolk amounted to no more than Norwich with its Castle Museum, Kings Lynn, and bleak Hunstanton, and she found this all rather repetitive – certainly not the sort of holiday for which Youth Hostelling had given her such a taste, nor even something to compare with more conventional family holidays by the beach. She had her way, and it was 1969 before we visited again. Meanwhile my uncle and aunt were politely disappointed, and I missed the flints, the strong smell of my uncle's pipe, my aunt's Lapsang Souchong tea, the reek of fishing nets and bracing winds off the North Sea, and the huge double bass called Fred which stood beside the stairs at 18 Market Place!

In 1958 we stayed in our first caravan, which was situated at Craigavan Holiday Camp, Sand Bay, near Weston. It was tiny and was provided with no cooking equipment other than a "Wee Baby Belling", which would have made preparing the Sunday lunch a problem, even if there had not been a power cut! Apart from that, I have a few clear memories: seeing a dead rat by the side of the road, when I went with my father to the local store, and the day when we took a boat trip from Weston Old Pier across the Channel to Penarth and back, and it poured with rain all the time. We did spend quite a lot of time on the beach at Marine Lake, where, by chance, we had met up with Audrey Hooper, who lived at Dorrington Terrace, not far from my grandparents' house, and whose sister, Dorothy, had been a very good friend of my mother during the war, but who, after being deserted by her husband, had died from TB in the early 50s, leaving a son, Peter, whom Audrey was bringing up. He became my playmate for the week. Nearly 30 years later he was to die, and his wife was to be made severely ill, as a result of carbon monoxide poisoning from a gas appliance at their home.

Another half-memory may be a trick of recollection: by chance, it was during our week in Weston that the composer, Vaughan Williams, died. I have an image of my father standing on the seafront at Anchor Head reading this news to me from his paper. Though I was soon to become precocious in the extreme where famous composers were concerned, at the age of five I neither knew about "classical music", nor about VW in particular. As ever, it seems my father was trying to interest me in things other parents (including my mother) would have considered inappropriate. Or was it that later, when studying music, I learned that Vaughan Williams had died whilst we were in Weston that year and my mind invented an image to go with the event?

There is another memory, and I do not know whether it belongs to Weston in 1958 or to our next holiday at Weymouth in 1960. In that year we took up the recommendation of our neighbour, Jean, and booked to stay at a rather better caravan camp at Littlesea near Weymouth. It was where Jean, Roger and Brenda stayed every year. There was a playground for children on the camp, not far from our caravan (or was it at Sand Bay? – this is the confusion). Though I frequented this all through the week, I did not integrate with the other children, despite my best attempts.

"Natter, natter, natter," they would say, when I appeared. "Natter, natter, natter!"

My father called their ringleader "The Pink Pig", which made me feel a bit better about myself.

Apart from that, I know in my bones that the first Weymouth holiday was a success – much more so than our stay at Sand Bay – though I don't recall precisely why that was so. The Weymouth holiday began well, when I avoided feeling sick on the coach by standing on the seat and thrusting my face into the small ventilating panel at the top of the window, so gaining fresh air and avoiding the billowing cigarette smoke in the coach itself. This made me feel blissfully happy, so much so that I sang Percy Faith's "Theme from a Summer Place" whenever we were passing through countryside and Mario Lanza's "Drink to Eyes" (to which I thought the words were "Drink, drink, drink, Eliza") as we passed through towns. Once we had arrived in Weymouth, the success of the holiday may have had something to do with my enchantment at the rhododendrons on the way to Lulworth Cove, and the strangeness of Portland Bill – then far less despoiled than it was later to become. Or maybe it was just the excellent beach and good weather. I do recall that all the time we were in Weymouth my mother was reading a book which they talked about on the wireless: "Lady Chatterley's Lover".

1962 saw us at Ringwood near Bournemouth, again in a caravan, but this time on a site surrounded with pinewoods. There was a rather good store where I purchased cartoon versions of "Julius Caesar" (later inflicted on Roger and Brenda) and "Macbeth", having recently watched "An Age of Kings" with my father. We also had a visit from the Packfords (my father's friends from Oxford), who knew the area well, even more importantly had a car, and were able during the course of one hectic Sunday to drive us around Poole and introduce us to the beach paradise of Sand Banks. John Packford also impressed us on that visit with his enthusiasm for Frank Ifield, who was currently No 1 with "I'll Remember You". (For several months Frank became our favourite too – until the Beatles came along.)

That holiday began with a triumph for me – one of which I never ceased to remind my parents during the holiday and for a long time afterwards. When we arrived by coach in Bournemouth, my parents needed a taxi to ferry us to the camp site. In the midst of blazing sunlight, a tumult of people, vehicles and exhaust fumes, neither of them could manage to flag one down. After about half an hour of frustration, I adopted my father's method of raising my right index finger in the air and fixing any potential driver with my questioning gaze, only to succeed in a very few minutes – probably because it looked so odd to see a nine-year-old doing this.

Those Summer holidays, together with our day trips with Maurice and by coach, were the extent of our travels as a young family living at Rodborough in the late '50s and early '60s. There was never any possibility that we would go abroad. We did not even dream of it. The only people we knew who went abroad were my mother's brother, Maurice, and my godmother, Joan Taylor. Maurice, who was 4 years younger than my mother, was unmarried and still lived at home with my grandparents. He had quite a good job as a draughtsman and must have had a reasonable salary, so due to that, combined with minimal living costs, he was able to afford to travel much more widely than anyone else in the family had ever done. Like my mother, he had become very keen on Youth Hostelling, but also mountaineering in the post WW2 era. This had led him to explore peaks in Wales and Scotland, but also to go as far as Switzerland. At the end of the '50s he started going on what a later generation would have called "lads' holidays" in Southern Spain with his friends, the Marriott brothers. The names of Torremolinos and Malaga became known to us, especially when Maurice came back with wine bottles in baskets and wall plates depicting bullfighting as presents, to say nothing of colour slides of beaches, bars and boozy ladies. A special evening would be arranged every so often for him to bring his colour slides, screen and projector to Rock Cottages for a viewing. (Until then we had never seen photographs which were not simply black and white prints from a box brownie.) Maurice was, in fact, a great enthusiast not only for hostelling and mountaineering, but also for photography and later cycling. His absorption in these passions perhaps explains why he remained unmarried for so long. In the early '60s he dated a girl from Gloucester, called Joy, to whom he became engaged. (My father went to the engagement party; my mother stayed home to look after myself and Ros.) The engagement did not last long, but within a few months he had introduced us to Marion Stevens, significantly younger than himself, but equally, if not more, passionate about walking, cycling and photography. They married about a year after we left Rodborough.

The other long-distance traveller of our acquaintance was Joan Taylor, who lived with her mother and stepfather (whom she always called "Mr Martin") in Horns Road – the same road in which my grandparents lived. She had become my mother's greatest friend at school (Stroud High School), and remained so during and after the War, and indeed for the rest of her life. She loved singing and light classics, was a soprano to my mother's contralto, and participated not only in the Ladies' Choir, Gilbert and Sullivan, and duetting with my mother, but also in the Trinity Church choir. She never married and, to my knowledge, never had a boyfriend. Indeed, in the most endearing way she was an "old maid", even when she was quite young. Unlike my mother, she had left school with qualifications and had obtained a good job with the Civil Service, working at various times in Swindon, at

Merrywalks in Stroud, and over at Elmore Court on the edge of Gloucester.

Living at home, therefore, with again few overheads, she, like Maurice, was able to afford travel abroad. Though she had gone hostelling and walking with my mother, physical exertion was not something she relished, and so holidays by train or coach to Switzerland or Austria appealed most to her, and I remember her coming up to my bedroom at Rodborough to tell me about a place called St Wolfgang and a building called "The White Horse".

Joan was someone whom we saw very frequently – at our house principally, but she would often be at my grandmother's particularly at Christmas. We rarely went to her house in Horns Road, but then again, it wasn't "her house", as such. I was invited in a few times, though, to see her budgerigar, Tommy Taylor, who used to recite his name and his address to all comers. Joan was a rather plump lady with a big bosom. My mother must have commented on this to me at some point, for the next time I saw Joan I transfixed her breast with my gaze till she blushed and asked me what was the matter. Fortunately, I had the presence of mind to say I was admiring her broach. Despite her singing and her voluminous chest, Joan always had trouble with her lungs. She was indeed "chesty" and had a piercing and high-pitched cough, which Ros and I would imitate. If she found something which I had said or done amusing, she also had a way of laughing and saying: "Oh – oh – oh – oh, Ma – a – a – a – r - tin!" – rather like Larry the Lamb on Children's Hour.

Compared to Joan and Maurice, we were little travelled as a family. Yet we travelled far more than the older generation. Neither Aunty Mue nor Aunty Gert, neither the Heavens nor the Gardies, ever took a holiday. From that point of view, my grandparents were quite adventurous. During the War for some reason a young woman – very much my mother's contemporary – was billeted for a while at Lower Lypiatt Terrace, though I can't imagine where she slept, unless her night shifts and my mother's were co-ordinated always to leave one bed free! This was Grace Burrows, who came from Exeter and whom we visited in 1955. At some point in the '50s my grandparents were persuaded that, since they knew Grace, they could easily catch a coach down to Exeter, stay with Grace's people and have a week's holiday in the process. This they did for a number of years and visited places in the Exeter area by bus. My grandfather was content as long as he "knew the ropes". In due course the Burrowses became too old to take guests and my grandparents went to a formal b&b, again not on the coast, but at Exeter, since that was what they knew – until the landlady also became too old, and at that point my grandparents' holidays ceased for good.

My grandparents' idea of a good day out or a holiday destination was somewhere where they could look at shop windows. Once, after Uncle Maurice had taken them out for the day to Wales, my grandfather lamented that there had been, "nothin' to see but miles and miles of mountains"!

As far as climbing mountains was concerned, my grandfather could see the point "if there was a crock of gold atop the mountain", but not otherwise!

As for foreign travel, he had been abroad in the tank corps at the end of World War 1 and had subsequently been to a place he pronounced as "Clone". He was less daunted by the distance involved in foreign travel than might have been imagined, and often quoted his neighbour, Banger Yates, who had once pronounced: "Paris? I could piss to Paris!"

Neither was there much experience of foreign travel where my father's family was concerned. My father himself had, of course, been abroad for most of the War in North Africa, Palestine and Italy, but never afterwards. His father had made one trip to Canada before I was born (why, in particular, I have no idea). Alice had been to Lourdes shortly after she converted to Catholicism, and Dorothy and Brian were taken to Paris by their daughter, Jane, and her husband, Clive, but apart from that never went anywhere other than the Norfolk coast (usually Blakeney), one trip to the Derbyshire Dales, and their regular visits to Gloucestershire.

Perhaps it was the unusualness and attraction of Summer holidays abroad which accounted for one of the most anguished experiences of my childhood. In 1963 malted-milk-voiced Cliff Richard's film, "Summer Holiday" came out, and many of the boys at school were taken to see it. I was told by my parents that I would be taken too, but something went wrong with the planning and the outing had to be called off. I have rarely felt so disappointed by anything else before or since!

CHAPTER 9

I have no memories of being ill as a baby at Lansdown, and my parents never referred later to my having required medical attention at that time. The only exception to this was the explanation given to me - in answer to what question? - that I had been circumcised for medical reasons. I do remember as a toddler suffering a minor injury when I was taken into the coal merchants' by my mother and Aunty Joan and managed to trap my fingers in the back of the large glass door, just as my mother attempted to close it! Even that did not necessitate a further trip to the hospital.

At Rodborough, however, I seemed to spend much time in my sick bed when I should otherwise have been at school, though perhaps memory has inflated the number of days involved. My colds were frequent, and Asian Flu packed me off to bed yet again in 1958. There were also the usual childhood infectious diseases: measles and chickenpox, and in the early '60s German Measles. At one point I had "swollen glands", but never mumps.

In an era when there was no vaccination against measles in particular, my parents' attitude to such illnesses seems in retrospect blasé. It boiled down to "Well, you're going to get it some time. It might as well be sooner than later. And if you can infect your sister at the same time, that's probably a good thing too!" But maybe the motive was to play down the known risks of such illnesses and to avoid alarming us. By contrast, the horrors of the illnesses for which you **could** have an injection by this period were stressed, particularly by my mother (with vivid accounts of cases of diphtheria in the virtual slum her family had inhabited during her infancy). The tactic there was obviously to make us all the more eager for "the needle"!

Other childhood ailments could usually be dealt with by a plaster and some Germolene, or by a drink of Lucozade! I did suffer at night with rheumatism (or what my parents said was rheumatism, though an earlier generation might have just called it "growing pains".) For this, my knees would be rubbed with Algepan, which had a pleasant odour, but made the flesh sting and burn, so that the original discomfort became masked and was forgotten.

Apart from German Measles, which came too late to have played any role, the infectious illnesses I contracted (together with my aversion to food) all encouraged my mother in her conviction that there was something fundamentally wrong with my tonsils and that these would simply have to come out! No amount of her daily administering of cod-liver oil, rosehip syrup, Parish's Food and Virol seemed to make any difference, and neither did the patent linctuses, Hill's Balsam, or the unspeakably foul-tasting Liquafruita, which I had to endure when a cold had actually taken grip.

My illnesses were always referred by my mother to her GP, Dr Newton, who had a surgery with a dingy waiting-room at the top of the town, which was shared with the more junior (and less intimidating) Dr McCrae. It was Dr Newton who eventually gave in to my mother's enthusiasm for a tonsillectomy. She placed enormous trust in his skills and judgement, and I learned later that when, following her marriage (or maybe her miscarriage), she had suffered mental problems (including the religious fixation), Dr Newton cured her, simply by taking time to talk to her and persuade her out of her obsessions. He was such a revered local figure that years later a new by-pass linking Wallbridge with Bowbridge was named after him.

Dr McCrae endeared himself to me, because he was good humoured and fun, and because his cough medicines tasted vastly sweeter than the Liquafruita, which my parents swore by. He became an even greater favourite once I had developed an interest in history and had been given a large book of historical facts and royal family trees. Calling at Rock Cottages to see me for my latest ailment, he seized upon this and devoted a surprising amount of time telling me all about the Scottish kings, and especially Malcolm Canmore, of whom previously I had never heard.

Another medic of whom I saw rather a lot was Mr Woodward at the Child Guidance Clinic, to which I was sent in the early '60s in an attempt to find out why I was still wetting the bed and to prevent it. He would talk to me as I drew or played with toys which he had provided, and made notes on what I did and said. These notes would then be passed under the door to a lady who would simultaneously be interviewing my mother in another room. I forget her name, but the fact that she had blue hair made an impression. Sadly, whatever therapy was being practised, it had no effect, and my mother continued to have mountains of bedding to wash every week for several more years.

The new decade of the '60s started momentously for me, for by then my mother had won over the sceptical Dr Newton and I had been referred to Stroud General Hospital. I'm fairly sure that it was on 11 January 1960 (the first date to engrave itself on my memory other than birthdays) that we caught the bus from Queen's Road with a small bag of essentials and made our way up through the town to the hospital. The prospect can't have worried me much, for as my mother and I walked up Middle Street towards our destination we bumped into my grandfather on his way back to work after lunch.

"I'm going to have my tonsils out," I enthused.

I seemed in fact to be entirely relaxed about what awaited me, even as we sat in the hospital entrance hall, which served as a waiting room (and reeked of ether), before being summoned forward for registration. The fact that the lady on reception was Vi Hamilton, a friend of my parents and of Aunty Joan Taylor, and that she made a fuss of me and said she would come to see me when I was on the ward, must have put me further at inappropriate ease.

The children's ward was on the first floor at the end of the building with windows looking out towards Rodborough and the lower part of the Stroud Valleys. I was given a bed on the right-hand side, and behind screens changed into a sort of a smock with a scarlet jacket, rather like the top half of a dressing-gown. The room contained about a dozen children of various ages, but none were much older than myself. In the next bed on my left was a boy called John Wager, whose birthday was the following day (the day of our operation) and who had a paltry array of pre-birthday cards beside his bed. We managed to converse in a friendly way, which was just as well, because before too long we were taken off to have a bath together! There were pleasant nurses, and an elderly lady patient who had a bed in a small alcove immediately adjacent, and who acted as a sort of grandmother figure, forever talking to and playing with the children, though I cannot remember her name. There was even a boy of my age on the other side of the ward whom I already knew from Sunday School: Simon Yates, who had suffered an appendicitis, the details of which he regaled me with, so that it became something I dreaded for the rest of my childhood. (The elderly lady patient had also suffered an appendicitis, and she told us how she had been singing a happy song as they took her stitches out, but I was not convinced!)

At some point it must have dawned on me in that my mother really had left me there and that for the first time in my life I would be without my parents for nearly a week. Certainly, I was as civil as a six-year-old could be when Vi Hamilton honoured her promise and came round to the ward to say hello again, but by the evening all had changed. Maybe my view of things altered when the previously pleasant nurses came round with a soapy solution which they stuck up our bums and immediately caused us to want to rush to the toilet. Whenever it was, by visiting time when my parents came to see me, I had sunken into despair. Though they chatted and tried to cheer me up, though my father had brought me a second-hand copy of "Treasure Island", it remained unopened on the bed, and I neither uttered a word nor even smiled at my parents, who had quite obviously abandoned me. A nurse tried to reassure my mother that there was nothing wrong and that my reaction was not unusual, and it was explained to me that the experience with the soapy water was merely to clear my system before the operation, but I remained desolate.

After my parents had left, lights out occurred very early, so that I then faced several hours of tossing and turning before I could go to sleep. Inevitably, I soon wanted to pee and so wandered down the ward in search of the night-nurse. When she saw me, I was scolded and told that I wasn't allowed out of bed. Small wonder that when I awoke very early the next morning my sheets were soaked. When this was discovered by one of the more elderly nurses, she let out a loud scream, and again I was told off, before I and the bed were stripped off and changed in full view of everyone else.

That rude awakening would have been around 6am. There was then a long wait before those of us who were going to have tonsillectomies (about half the ward) were due to have our operations. It had been made clear to us that at that point we could neither eat nor drink, but both John Wager and I felt very thirsty and began whimpering about it. The old lady patient took pity and said that surely a little water wouldn't hurt, and went to fetch us glasses of water whilst the nurses weren't watching. When eventually it was my turn to go down to theatre and I was moved from my bed to a trolley, a plastic hood, again reeking of ether, was placed over my hair. Whether it was that smell, or whether it was my alarm at having breached regulations by drinking water, or whether it was the water itself on top of whatever medication I had been given, I vomited before we had even left the ward. The day was not off to a good start.

I had no particular sense of fear when I was wheeled before the surgeon, and I started to count to ten, when he requested me to do so……..

My next clear memory was of regaining consciousness back in the children's ward and seeing heavy snow falling outside the windows opposite my bed. My parents were not allowed to visit for 24 hours, but I must have slept a lot that day and would not have been much more welcoming than I had been the evening before.

The rest of the week proceeded as something of a blur. Snow continued to fall from time to time. My parents' visits resumed, and I was kinder to them. Several times I suffered the ordeal of being found to have wet the bed and being made to feel guilty about it. As a child who was difficult about food at the best of times, I worried about mealtimes, and was not in any way attracted to the soft foods (stewed meat, mashed potatoes, ice cream, and blancmange) which we were given. I was told that I would probably have a sore throat, though I did not seem to have one. What I did notice was that my nose was bleeding – something which was explained when my mother found out and told me that my adenoids had been whipped out at the same time as my tonsils. This was a surprise, especially as I had no previous awareness of owning such a thing as an adenoid.

In retrospect, what is more noteworthy is not what I do remember, but what I do not. In the years which followed the operation I very soon developed an antipathy to syringes and an even more overwhelming fear of blood. It first manifested itself a year or so later when I pulled out a tooth and almost fainted at the slight smear of blood this produced. I also had to lie down when, as we listened to "Two Way Family Favourites" over lunch one Sunday, they played Tony Hancock's "The Blood Donor" and the reference to "a whole arm-full" almost floored me. This issue became such a problem in later life that I would frequently faint after a blood test, and was so agitated on one occasion before a small dental operation that the dentist had to decline to proceed. Several times I had therapy for this. Only the last therapist latched on to the idea that the phobia might have been something to do with the tonsillectomy. She told me that wards where that operation was carried out could be very bloody places, as she could attest from her early nursing career. Maybe I saw something which horrified me. It's strange that though I remember John Wager, I have no memory of whoever it was that occupied the bed on my right. Maybe they bled. Why do I recall in such detail most of what happened on the first day or so, and so little afterwards? Whatever the case, once the connection had been made by the therapist, I will not say I was cured of my phobia, but it affected me less.

At the end of the week, it was by no means confirmed that I would be going home – another cause for anxiety, but when my mother came in on the Friday or Saturday morning it was finally conceded that we could climb into the ambulance taking us and various other ex-patients to our respective homes.

There was then still much snow on the ground, and it remained for quite a while afterwards. Following my operation, I had to stay in bed at home for four weeks before returning to school. At one point I was shaken when there seemed to be a loud explosion at my bedroom window. Ernie Gardiner had thrown a snowball at it - as a joke! The rest of my convalescence, however, passed without incident, and was really rather tedious. But at least I was home, and my parents were forgiven. Ernie was forgiven too when he let me have an enormous and very ancient wireless set, which, from then on, was a permanent and much used feature of my bedroom, the likes of "Grand Hotel" and "Desert Island Discs" easing the boredom of subsequent illnesses.

There is no doubt that my experience of hospitalisation in the early '60s was fairly traumatic, but I should be grateful it was not worse. During a subsequent house-clearance, my mother found correspondence which related to Aunty Alice's first of many spells in hospital half a century earlier. In particular, there was a letter from the matron to Alice's mother from which it is clear that a child of no more than one or two years of age was sent to a hospital in a different town (Gloucester) and kept there with no parental visits at all for two weeks. Throughout the letter Alice was referred to, not by her name, but as "baby".

Author's Mum, Dad and Joan in "The Mikado" 1949

Author's Dad in Olivier style

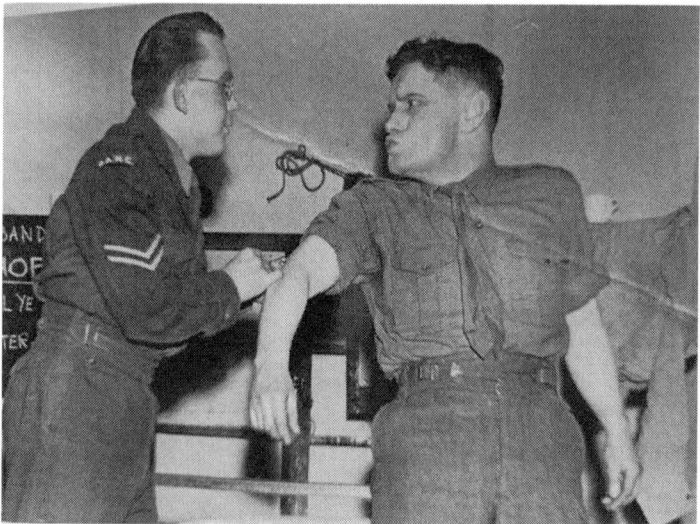

Author's Dad in "Reluctant Heroes"

Author's Dad and his sister, Nancy

Author and his sister, Ros - about 35 years later

Ros and author at the gate to 4 Rock Cottages, with Rodborough Fort in the background

Author's Mum and Joan Taylor in their hostelling days

Family group outside 17 Lower Lypiatt Terrace: (left to right) Gramp, Dad, me, Mum, Ros, Gran.

Roger and author

Roger, Brenda and the author eating ice cream outside Rock View

Author and his sister Ros sitting over the coal hole outside 4 Rock Cottages

The White Family in the garden of 17 Lower Lypiatt Terrace

Market Place, Swaffham

Caravan camp at Sand Bay, Weston-super-Mare.

CHAPTER 10

Back at school, the remainder of that academic year passed without memorable incident, other than our week's holiday at Weymouth at Whitsun, and my mother's bout of indecision over which primary school to send me to. September was another matter, though, for it was then that I became a pupil at Church Street Boys' School in the centre of Stroud.

The school occupied a purpose-built Cotswold Stone building which bore the date 1883 over its main entrance. It was roughly in the shape of a squat "H", of which the right-hand downward stroke ran parallel with Ryeleaze Road. The main door, together with two classrooms and a washroom, were on the right of the "H", whereas its left comprised another two classrooms, plus the headmaster's office and another washroom. The central section (parallel with Brick Row) was occupied by the school hall and behind it a long corridor joining the two wings of the building.

Behind the central section of the school was a small yard with a storeroom for PE (or "PT", as we called it then) and a bicycle shed. The very large main playground was, however, on the left of the building, and this sloped from the back (near the cycle sheds) down to a high corrugated iron fence, behind which was Holloway's factory (workplace at various times of my grandfather, mother, and Aunty Gert). There was also a rectangular yard in front of the school, linking the main playground to the school gate, which was on Ryeleaze Road.

The school was at a higher level than Holloway's, but much of the tall factory buildings could be seen from the playground protruding way above the corrugated iron fence. Those factory buildings ran all along the side of the main playground, but did not overlap with the school buildings themselves. There were some offices belonging to the factory at a lower level, more or less opposite the main school door, but these were not visible from the school. They had a flat asphalt roof, which appeared to be an extension of the playground area, but upon this it was forbidden to walk, play, or do anything else – presumably because the weight of several dozen schoolboys might have caused it to collapse! Immediately adjacent to that roof area was the school flagpole from which the Union Jack was flown by the headmaster on royal birthdays and Commonwealth Day. Not far away, but on the other side of the metal fence, was the factory whistle, the piercing noise of which punctuated our schooling several times each day.

Towards the higher end of the main playground were the redbrick toilets (a urinal and about six closets), and adjacent to them was a long, low and rather more modern building, which was the canteen. It had a broad flight of steps up to its main entrance. Sickening smells emanated from it, and in particular from its drains, which were caked with the detritus of school dinners. It had large windows overlooking the playground all along one side, but because of the risk that these would be smashed by misdirected footballs, a metal framework had been erected in front, reinforced with a covering of chain-linked wire. The lower half of the framework below the windows was open and unencumbered with this protective covering, and, since there was also a small ledge at about one foot above ground level running along the front of the building itself, this provided the opportunity for boys to swing from the framework backwards and forwards to the ledge: something I found myself doing many times in my first year at the school, whenever I had no one to talk to or nothing else in particular to do.

At the far end of the playground beyond the canteen there were some large wooden sheds and an area where coke for the boilers was stored. The fearsome climbing frames which were used for PT were stored within the sheds, though that cannot have been their only purpose, and I never knew whether they belonged to the school or to the factory. Beside and behind the sheds there was a further extent of tarmac, which might have been intended as an extension of the playground at one time, but had become another forbidden zone, presumably because any boy who was tempted to go there would be out of sight of the school staff. There would always be a master on duty during playtimes watching out for misdemeanours, but at lunchtime this role would be taken by the very Mrs Seymour with the two sets of false teeth who was my grandmother's friend. Once as we waited to go into the canteen, Mrs Seymour hauled out and (despite his protestations) reprimanded a boy for allegedly pushing her. This was Philip Pickett, later to find fame and then sadly notoriety with the New London Consort.

There are two political events which I associate with the playground at Church Street Boys' School. The first must have been in my very first term, when the American Presidential election was held, and my mother had explained to me that it was a contest between a millionaire's son and the son of a grocer. I was accosted in the playground by an older boy who demanded to know which of them I supported. Some sense of class loyalty drove me to say the grocer's son, which was the right answer, and I was allowed to go about my business unpummelled.

The second event also involved Kennedy, namely the Cuban Missiles Crisis of Autumn 1962. The crisis must have been at its height, for those boys who had gone home for dinner (myself included) on one particular day came back to the playground convinced that World War III was upon us, and, as the word spread, a hush fell on the school yard and boys went into huddles to discuss our imminent doom. Mrs Seymour, who was not in on the news, was mystified and was heard to say: "I don't know what on earth they be a-talkin' about!"

When I started at the school, Roger was still a pupil, though, being three years older than me, he was in Standard 4, the most senior class. On my first day he showed me round the outside of the school and at playtime introduced me to the delights of swinging from the bars outside the canteen, but, having performed his neighbourly duty, soon left me there and drifted away to join his peers. (Childhood friendship was very much a function of a particular environment!) After a day or two of disconsolate swinging, I noticed another lost looking waif outside the canteen. This was Michael Toft, who became my best friend for the whole time I was a pupil at Church Street. At first, we used to swing in consort until it was time to rejoin lessons. Later, we would instead spend playtimes and lunchtimes deep in conversation about our favourite topics (great composers and history), or at least I would talk, and he would listen. ("Natter, natter, natter," you might say.) There was a particular nook just inside the school gate to which we would resort and which we called "Composer Corner".

There must have been many interactions with other pupils: just chatting and fooling around, but I was never one for joining ball games. Later, playing conkers might attract me, or swapping bubble gum cards – flags of the world (with basic facts about each country on the reverse) became a particular favourite. There was even a craze once for constructing and flying very light balsawood planes. I joined in, only for my plane to disintegrate on its first flight. Lecturing Michael was a more congenial use of time!

The first formal activity of the school day (repeated at the end of each playtime and after lunch) was for us to line up in the yard in our respective years at right-angles to the school, with the most senior pupils at the upper end nearest the cycle sheds, below whom stood in order first Standard 3, then Standard 2, then Standard 1, each class in one long line. A master would then position himself in front of the seniors and bark commands to the whole school: "Atten-TION...Stand at - EASE...Atten-TION...Stand at - EASE...Atten-TION...LEFT - TURN...Left, right, left, right, left, right", and at that point the most junior boys (followed by the other years in turn) would march off in formation to the steps leading up to the main school door. As first year pupils, we would then cross a red tiled hall adjacent to the washroom, march along a dark passage beside the school hall, and then turn right into the Standard 1 classroom.

This was a comparatively small square room with high windows. There were desks for about 20-25 boys arranged in rows facing the teacher and the blackboard, with our backs to the main windows. They were metal-framed wooden desks with a sloping top and a shelf beneath on which to rest books and paper. The whole assemblage was bolted together with a narrow seat and was very difficult to move about. Whatever the methodology behind the allocation of desks that first day, I ended up towards the back of the form on the left, next to a boy called Stephen Pearce.

The teacher whom we then all faced was Mr Campbell, a tall lugubrious looking man with a florid complexion, grey hair and always a grey suit. He had an agreeable smell, which in due course I discovered to be the smell of alcohol from the pub on the Bath Road where he would spend lunchtimes, when not "on duty". It amused him, for some reason, to refer to me as "Martin Luther White", and he was generally well disposed towards me. Early on, though, he decided to separate me from Stephen Pearce, when he suspected (correctly) that I had copied the answer to the question: "What is the modern name of Russia?" in a general knowledge test. Nobody else in the form had a clue, and it must have seemed strange that we both gave the answer "URSS"! I felt humiliated and never did such a thing again.

CHAPTER 11

The fascination with great composers, which I shared with Michael Toft, arose, in my case, from my parents' purchase of a second-hand piano early in 1961. It was acquired for a very low price from a couple called the Everetts, who lived along Rodborough Lane above the Tabernacle. The instrument was placed along the inner wall of our living room, just to the right of the door as you went in.

Previously my only involvement with the performing arts had been when I was given first a drum and then a triangle to "play" in the infant school band. Even I could tell that I was hopeless at both, and it was a further indignity when my mother told me that she had had to play the triangle at school, and that it was the instrument they gave you if you could do nothing else!

The first task after the installation of the piano was to have it tuned, and this was done by Jimmy Goodman, a trained (but largely unemployed) classical pianist, who sometimes accompanied my mother and Aunty Joan in their duets. He spent a couple of hours tinkering with the instrument's innards, and, whilst he was working, showed me how he used a tuning fork. He managed to return the piano to a playable state, except with regard to one of the white keys (it may have been the D above Middle C), which continued to stick when played, and for which the damper never worked. It had an acerbic tone, which provided a sort of drone effect for whatever piece was being performed, but one got used to it.

Next, my parents set about arranging piano lessons for me, and again it was to Jimmy Goodman that they turned. On 21st March 1961 (the date was at the top of page 1 of my music homework notebook) I had my first lesson with him at Cartref, Bowbridge Lane, not far from my grandparents' house. Jim was kindly and himself very talented, but he was not a trained teacher. He lived with his mother (the controlling Mrs Crosby), had strange white deposits in his ears and an ever-rumbling tummy. Despite this, in no time, I became very enthusiastic about the piano and classical music in general.

To bolster my burgeoning interest, my father shared with me his Observer Book of Music, which was a short guide to musical terms and history, with potted biographies of the great composers from Albeniz to Wolf. This I pored over and inwardly absorbed, sufficiently for me to test Michael Toft on his knowledge of their lives and works during our lunch hours. Michael was also learning the piano, but sadly for him did not have access to the Observer Guide!

Until then, my taste in music had been determined by what I heard on the Light Programme and the songs my mother sang in the kitchen. My first favourite song was "Pickin' A Chicken" recorded by Eve Boswell – but also sung by Phyllis White, with me in her arms joining in the chorus. I had become aware too of something called Skiffle, which seemed to dominate an unlistenable programme, "Saturday Club" with Brian Matthew. More to my taste on a Saturday morning was "Children's Favourites" with Uncle Mack. He could be relied on to play something by Tommie Steele at approximately 9.55am, which was always my father's cue (before he had to work on Saturdays at "The Citizen") to escape to Stroud to do some shopping. I knew of Dickie Valentine, of Harry Belafonte's "Scarlet Ribbons" and of another singer called Michael Holliday, whom I was once taken to see, starring with Lita Rosa, in pantomime at Gloucester. At the age of 5, I used to sing one of his hits, "The Story of My Life", which for some reason my father found hilarious. Sadly, the story of Michael Holliday's life came to an early close when he committed suicide a few years later.

After the acquisition of the piano, all of this was to change, and I wished to listen to nothing but the Third Programme (whilst I leafed through The Observer Guide). My obsession was further fed by my father, who introduced me to the Promenade concerts, the first half an hour of which I was allowed to listen to before bed, and by Aunty Dorothy and Uncle Brian, who were only too delighted that I had begun piano lessons and was becoming involved with their own great passion. I started writing to them every month or so to tell them about my lessons. It seems they were all the more interested, since there was a romantic attachment between Jim Goodman and Brian's younger sister, Joyce, though later this was stamped upon by Mrs Crosby and the equally controlling Mrs Bowle, mother of Brian and Joyce. The holidays to Norfolk in 1961 and 1963, of course, gave added impetus to my passion, and I was introduced to music I would never have discovered otherwise, such as Mozart's 23rd Piano Concerto in A. Even my mother liked that one.

Yet all was not quite as it seemed, at least after my first rush of enthusiasm for classical music. Although I announced that I wished to become a composer, imagined myself dying Romantically of consumption, and indeed started scrawling little tunes in music score, which my father bought for me at Stroud Music Centre on the London Road, I was, to be honest, not particularly good either at playing or at composition. Besides, as my mother later told me, although she had allowed my father and Aunty Joan to influence her into taking an interest in the lighter classics, that was not where her own real passion lay. There were the songs from the '30s – '50s sung in the kitchen whilst she worked. She also introduced me to the Light Programme's "Pick of the Pops" with Alan Freeman on Sunday afternoons, and this we would listen to, whether we were home at 4 Rock Cottages or at my grandparents' house. Most subversive of all was her introduction to me, via the television, of the new craze for The Twist as promoted by Mr Chubby Checker!

I began to lead a double life, keeping up with my piano lessons, writing to Dorothy and Brian, and talking composers to Michael Toft: all activities I considered to be virtuous, whilst at the same time harbouring a growing and at times, I felt, shameful interest in the Top 10 and, from early 1963 onwards in The Beatles! Once we had left Rodborough in June 1963 and my piano lessons had come to an end (temporarily), the popular strain became dominant. So began an alternation between cultural imperatives which dominated my life for the next thirty years!

As for the Beatles themselves, "Love Me Do" did not register with me, but once I'd heard "Please, Please Me" on "Two Way Family Favourites", I was fascinated – even if confused, since I thought the boys' falsettos were girls' voices. During my eleventh year, as hit followed hit, I became more and more involved, and whilst for a long time my father feigned abhorrence (as he always did for pop culture), my mother and sister became enthusiastic too. Even my father was won over in the end.

With regard to my interest ("our", if you include Michael Toft) in history, it was something which had been encouraged as the family made trips to the odd castle or two (Norwich, Berkeley and, on a more modest scale, Sandsfoot near Weymouth). Then, when I joined Mr Campbell's class, we were each allocated a book which had a picture of a centurion on the cover, and which told Britain's story in anecdotes about figures deemed of interest to 8–year-olds. For some reason, there was a chapter about Queen Matilda (in the broad sweep of history, hardly the most important of medieval personalities), and Erasmus was there too, whilst yet another chapter concerned "Tar Macadam" and his roads. However, what really ignited my fascination with the subject was again my father's perhaps inappropriate (but in this case accurate) assumptions as to what an 8 –year-old could comprehend. He let me join him week after week after Sunday dinner to watch the BBC's "Age of Kings", which comprised all of Shakespeare's history plays, other than "King John" and "Henry VIII". So captivated was I by the stories and the characters and the murders, that I would spend the rest of my Sunday afternoon (if we were not going to Horns Road) reading and rereading more factually based accounts in my encyclopaedia: "The Book of Knowledge".

This series of tomes was another contribution by Aunty Dorothy and Uncle Brian to my intellectual development. They had given it initially to their own daughter, Jane, presumably in the 1940s. When she had finished with it, it was passed to her cousin, Colin Walker, who lived at Amberley, and later played cello in the Electric Light Orchestra and the Covent Garden Orchestra. It then came to me and my sister for a few years, before again being collected and given to Jane's sons, Trevor and Peter. It must have comprised at least six substantial volumes, quite expensively bound in maroon and gold covers. Having been compiled in the '30s, it contained sections on countries (such as Latvia and Lithuania) which I had never heard of, because they did not exist as independent states by my time, and for history it rather petered out with the rise of Hitler and Mussolini. However, for earlier history it was invaluable to me. To its final volume, I paid little attention at first. It was sub-titled "Index" and had a section explaining what events had happened on each day in the year, and then a much longer section which was indeed an index, but an index with detailed notes.   For instance, under "Russia" it listed all the Tsars and their dates, and many other countries had similar lists. It even had a list of all the popes since St Peter! Once I realised what it contained, it became my bible, and lists of kings, lists of my favourite this and my favourite that, and family trees both real and imagined filled my notebooks. When asked to contribute something to place on the wall of my classroom (by then that of Standard 2) for a parents' evening, I produced the queen's genealogy going right back to Egbert. Imagine my joy when I discovered a book for children at the local lending library entitled "Blood Royal" by the Moncrieff of Moncrieff, which contained simplified family trees for most of the royal houses of Europe and even beyond!

In so far as lighter reading was concerned, I continued year after year to enjoy perusing the Rupert annual, but after youthful dalliance with comics such as "Playhour" and the spin-off, "Harold Hare's Pet's Club", I was never given the opportunity of reading the more hardcore "Dandy" and "Beano", though I would sneak a look at Roger and Brenda's copies. Likewise, my parents never offered to provide me with "Look and Learn" or "Knowledge", presumably because they thought it an unnecessary expense, if I was already enthused by encyclopaedias and "Blood Royal"!

CHAPTER 12

The curriculum in Mr Campbell's class was much more focused than it had been at the infant school, and there were certainly no more nature walks! There was, of course, our history textbook, and we also spent a lot of time drawing silhouettes: black against yellow, red against black and so on. There must also have been a smattering of geography, nature study and PT, but the Three Rs, and in particular reading, became my major priority. It was probably not Mr Campbell himself, but it may have been Roger who gave rise to the belief - or maybe it was just a rumour which went round the form - but the received wisdom from the outset was that, if you hadn't learned to read properly within two weeks, you would have to go and see "Joner"!

"Joner" was Mr Rhys-Jones, the Headmaster: a tall imposing man with a rather round flat face, and grizzled greying hair. He was reputed to be very strict and was known to use the cane. Though it was difficult to reconcile the two images, I had also heard from my mother's friend, Joan Skinner, that Joner was something called a Freemason, and that he had been seen at the Subscription Rooms (where there must have been a Masonic temple) wearing a pinny with his trouser leg rolled up. Unable to credit the latter picture, I put it from my mind and contented myself with being terrified.

Fear reaped its reward. Within two weeks of my joining the form I had made more progress with reading than I had in several years under the ministrations of Miss Bowering and my parents' attempts to make me read "Janet and John" books. I became so adept that before long Mr Campbell asked me to try to impart some of my skill to one of the more desperately backward boys in the form, a sad individual, who smelled of urine, spoke in no more than a mumble and before the end of the year had been taken away to a "special school". Additional responsibility landed on my shoulders later in the year, when I became the "monitor" charged with taking the daily register for inspection by Mr Rhys-Jones. This meant rapping on the door of the classroom where he taught the top form, interrupting his lesson, and waiting by his desk as he perused the attendances. On one of the earliest occasions when I undertook this task, he asked me if I was scared of him, so audible must have been the knocking of my knees. I assured him I was not.

Terrified into an ability to read, I availed myself of the various reading materials provided for Mr Campbell's form. There was a series of short stories about pirates, each of whom had a passion for a particular type of gemstone and spent their whole time sailing around the Caribbean in quest of whatever jewel it was. Then there were tales from Greek mythology, but also Norse tales about the likes of Odin, Loki, and Baldur the Beautiful, which I particularly enjoyed.

So improved were my reading skills that before long I had joined the junior section of Stroud Library in Lansdown. Apart from gorging myself vampire-like on "Blood Royal", I devoured a whole series of books for children on the great composers. These had rather twee titles like "Mozart the Wonder Boy", "Ludwig van Beethoven and the Chiming Tower Bells", and "Robert Schumann and Mascot Ziff". There were history books too, which introduced me to French history, and then the French and Russian Revolutions. An interest in Egyptology was spawned when I read a book called "Land of the Pharaohs" by Leonard Cottrell.

At home there was already a set of Richmal Crompton's William books (inherited from my father and Aunty Alice), which I read and re-read, despite the suggestion at one point that they were a bad influence on me! I also began to collect Enid Blyton's "Famous Five" and "Adventure" books, the Worzel Gummidge stories and Gwynedd Rae's now forgotten, but delightful "Mary Plane" series. I was particularly fond of the Blyton "Adventure" series, and on occasions stayed in bed on a Sunday till I had read an entire volume. "The Circus of Adventure" had the author toying with her own Ruritania, which she called Tauri Hessia, of which the rightful king was a boy called Aloysius, for some reason billeted on the usual child heroes. I became obsessed with Aloysius and his plight and imagined myself comforting him and wiping away his tears! I started inventing countries of my own, though they quickly evolved from cod Mitteleuropa to a clutch of Anglo-Saxon fiefdoms!

Even after I had learned to read well, my parents would still occasionally read to me, and in this way I became acquainted with "Tom Sawyer" and "Huckleberry Finn", though my mother struggled to render the Mississippi dialogue in a way which satisfied her, steeped though she was in American film culture.

Of the little boys in Standard 1, other than my rather sad reading student, perhaps the most exotic was Giovanni Lugomasini, who spoke strangely and had an accent which I had never heard before. He was friendly, if rather brusque, and said he had learned English from a big book. I once asked him to teach me a word in Italian, which he did, and I treasured the word "vento" (wind) for more than 40 years, until I at last took formal lessons in the language! Then there was Stephen Pearce, who seemed very bright and intelligent, but after I had been removed from his ambit, due to the cheating incident, I was placed next to one of the form's willy fiddlers. When one day in a fit of self-righteousness I hit out at him on account of his latest revelation, I managed to give him a black eye, but he never divulged to his parents or to Mr Campbell who had done this – probably for fear of being asked what had provoked the attack in the first place! Whilst I was still sitting next to Stephen Pearce we had both spied another boy who took an embarrassing interest in his own anatomy. When Stephen informed me that this boy was playing with his "penny", I repeated this to my parents, who then felt obliged to show me the word "penis" in the dictionary, together with its formal definition as "the typical male organ".

Of course, Michael Toft was my best friend, and he was definitely not a willy fiddler. Together we managed to survive the cold grey lunch times and playtimes, united in our interests which, particularly as far as music was concerned, we seemed to share with no one else. Nobody in our form ever mentioned playing an instrument, and no musical tuition was offered by the school. Indeed, there was no choir or communal singing, other than during morning assembly. (It may have been Mrs Rhys-Jones who played the piano on those occasions, though it was probably her multi-tasking husband himself.) The only musical education during my whole three years at the school revolved around the educational radio broadcast, "Singing Together" with William Appleby, for which each year there was a booklet of songs, such as "Hearts of Oak",

"Camp Town Races", and "Polly Oliver", which we would learn in class. That said, in those days music (other than singing) was something extracurricular and the prime responsibility of parents, and so was not something which pupils or masters ever discussed. Certainly, two boys who joined my form after that first year went on to have professional musical careers, and yet I never knew till many years later that they had any interest in the subject. In the year above there was also the later disgraced Philip Pickett.

Some months after I had first made Michael Toft's acquaintance, he handed to me an envelope addressed to my mother. It turned out to be a letter from his mother saying, that, since we two boys had so much in common, perhaps our friendship should be extended outside the school environment. So it was that a series of exchange visits commenced on Saturday afternoons. One week I would go by bus to Chalford and would walk up a very steep hill to his parents' house. There we would play the piano (after a fashion), go for walks, swing on a rope suspended from a tree in the garden, and have tea, before I skipped down the hill to catch the 5.10 back to Rodborough. A week or two later he would come to our house, again for piano playing, games on the Common, and for tea.

Poor Michael! He was very shy. On one of his visits, we dashed up to the Common after tea, before he was due to catch his bus. When we dashed back a little late, he was too reticent to say he wanted to pee, so I rushed him down to the bus stop, where, before the bus arrived a wet patch suddenly spread across the front of his shorts. On another occasion, standing in the same place on the bus stop a bird shat upon his head. I was not sympathetic on either occasion, and told our friends at school all about what had befallen "Toffee", as we called him!

One Saturday when I was at Michael 's house, we decided to go for a walk with his older sister. In their own environment they seemed to have no fear, and I followed in trepidation as they led me across a field known to contain adders. We then spent several blissful hours in a builder's yard, taking turns to roll down a bank inside a large metal bin, and then dammed an adjacent stream with bags of cement, which were lying about. Eventually, we heard a church clock chiming five, which was a disaster, since I was due to catch my usual bus home and we hadn't even had tea yet! My parents had no phone for us to contact and, of course, my mother would be "frantic". After a rushed tea, Mr Toft drove me down to the bus stop and I arrived home an hour late. There were recriminations and scoldings, but they had blown over by the following day. I often wondered if the flooding of the builder's yard, due to our activities, was resolved as quickly.

If my interactions with the other pupils (amounting in the case of Michael Toft to a friendship of sorts, or at the least a mutual dependence) mitigated the rather cheerless atmosphere of Church Street Boys' School, one aspect of our day-to-day lives blighted my existence to such an extent that it made me thoroughly miserable, and that was the necessity of eating school dinners. I had always been difficult to feed, and even after my mother's panacea of the tonsillectomy, I was still extremely finicky. Unfortunately, Church Street was quite a distance from Rodborough and the only solution to the need for nourishment in the middle of the day seemed to be for my mother to pay the five shillings a week required for me to have school dinners in the canteen. They were pretty poor fare. The least objectionable would be a salad of lettuce leaves with lumpy mashed potatoes and a slice of luncheon meat. But so often the lumpy mashed potatoes were accompanied instead by a thin fatty stew of carrots, pieces of unidentifiable meat and some form of grain or lentils. I would eat a few mouthfuls and then push the remainder of the meal to one side of the plate, so that it would appear I had eaten far more than I had. On occasions, even the most undiscriminating of the pupils would rebel and refuse to eat what was put in front of them, and this once produced threats from the duty master that anyone who did not eat up would have to see the Headmaster and "stay in after school". How I evaded that punishment I cannot remember, but I do remember on another occasion a pudding was served which comprised a rock-hard biscuit, a lump of blancmange and what I was convinced was a pickled onion, but which in retrospect was probably an olive. The prospect of eating an onion for pudding so horrified me that I began to cry, at which point a boy called Gerry Brown, who was sitting opposite me and who was the naughtiest boy in the form, offered to eat my pudding for me. So relieved was I, that I gave him sixpence from my pocket-money: the value of the sweet course.

"Caw! A whole tanner," he said, and there began a most unlikely alliance, which led to my being invited to Gerry Brown's birthday party about eighteen months later. Gerry's family lived at the top of the town, and, as Gerry and his posse of friends (including me) ascended the hill after school, it was impressed on all of us that no one was to utter a word about "What I'm like", as Gerry put it. Apparently, on a previous occasion James Ward (who was also part of the contingent) had blabbed about Gerry's bad behaviour and had suffered the consequences the next day: a painful experience, as James was ready to acknowledge. The apotheosis of my friendship with Gerry Brown would not, however, occur until my final year at Church Street.

I endured school dinners for the whole of my first year at Church Street, and for part of the second. At that point, the combination of my heartfelt complaints and the fact that I would often come home from school with a severe headache, either from stress or lack of food, persuaded my mother (who sympathised, because she too suffered from "bilious headaches") to devise an alternative strategy. This meant, in the first place, that on Mondays and Wednesdays I would rush out of school after morning lessons and make my way as quickly as I could on foot all the way back to 4 Rock Cottages (through Stroud and up Rodborough Hill), where a cooked dinner would be awaiting me and which I would bolt down, before running down to the bus stop to catch the 1.10 back into Stroud.

On Tuesdays and Thursdays I would instead go to my grandmother's, where I would be fed a hearty stew (complete with bullet –like dumplings); or a charred, but delicious slice of steak with chips which were black and limp after prolonged frying in dripping; or, best of all, grandma's rissoles, which were a combination of mashed potato, minced beef and sage, formed into a dome and baked again with lots of beef dripping, so that the outside was thick and crunchy. Neither my mother, nor I in due course, ever managed to replicate this culinary marvel.

The last element of my mother's plan of campaign was for me to go to Aunty Joan Skinner's on Fridays. Joan and her husband, Stan (a childhood friend of my father's), lived in Lansdown, quite close to the school. There the fare was more basic: often pale fatty chips and rather pink sausages, but the welcome was warm, and it was far preferable to staying at the canteen. The Skinners had five children, and, though the eldest, Martin, was now at secondary school, there would always be various of his sisters, or his baby brother present to play with. At one point they also had a dog called Jip, who was extremely boisterous. With little experience of dogs, I found him intimidating and would try to fend him off.

"He's not used to it, Mart," said Aunty Joan on one occasion.

"Well, nor am I," I blurted out in reply.

"You don't *have* to come here, Martin," was the rejoinder, which, with its implied threat of a return to the school canteen, was enough for me to redouble my efforts to befriend Jip, or at least endure his leapings up and slobberings. Fortunately, this was not for long, since Jip became so big and so boisterous that in the end even the Skinner family was glad to see him rehomed!

Apart from Aunty Joan Taylor, the Skinners and John and Peggy Packford were the only friends of my parents that my sister and I ever encountered on a regular basis. We would exchange occasional Sunday visits with the Skinners, and the Packfords would drive over from Oxford for an afternoon, or collect our whole family to spend a weekend with them at their house in Divinity Road. On one of the trips to Oxford we were all taken to Abingdon Airport on a particularly cold and grey afternoon (though it can only have been September). There was some talk of the boys being taken up in an aeroplane – an idea which filled me with horror – but, fortunately, it didn't materialise. Back at Divinity Road – I think my father and Uncle John must have been out at the pub – his wife, Peggy, showed my mother her collection of dresses, which I thought quite a strange thing to do (as did my mother), but then we watched the Last Night of the Proms, which, at that time in my life, I thought was wonderful and made up for the rest of the day.

Other aspects of visits to the Packfords of which I have vague recollections: the frequent visits of Peggy's father, who had the phlegmiest cough you every heard; the presence in the house of one

Miss Fox, whose role I never quite worked out; a pissing competition with Andrew, the Packfords' elder son; and the huge map they had on their dining room wall showing the British Empire in the usual pink/red colour, which filled us with wonder.

There was one other set of my parents' friends who made an impression on me at this time, and they were a family I met only once: the Stickles family from South Africa. I can only speculate that my father had become acquainted with them during the early part of the War, when his regiment had had to stop off in Cape Town on its way to invade Egypt. The family comprised Charles, his wife, Bill, and their daughter, who was roughly my age and was called Bonny. They came to tea at 4 Rock Cottages bringing a relative of theirs who lived in Gloucester and whose existence was probably the main reason for their visit to England. Two aspects of that day stand out. In the first place, Charles was very taken with me, and talked in quite a serious way of my visiting them in South Africa, and swimming in their pool: a prospect which alarmed me even more than going up in an aeroplane, and certainly alarmed my mother. The second aspect related to their fulsome commiserations with their Gloucester relative at the amount she had to pay for coal, when compared with the prices they were used to themselves. This caused my mother (after they had left) to say that, of course, in this country we didn't rely on slave labour in our mines: a radical pronouncement for her, given her usual political standpoint!

CHAPTER 13

My daily trip to school took me on foot from Rock Cottages to the Pike and then all the way down Rodborough Hill, past rows of mainly terraced houses on the left, past the Co-op at Spillman's Road also on the left, my old infant school on the right, then over the railway bridge and down to the Bath Road.

Often in the early days this descent and the rest of the journey was made with Roger and/ or Brenda, though, after Roger had progressed to the Archway Secondary Modern, I would also often walk in company with Janice and Mary Young, two twins whom I had known at infant school, who lived just below the Prince Albert, and who were now being educated at Castle Street Girls' School. They were not identical twins, but always dressed in matching blue macs. Since they were the only twins I knew, I did not object to their failure to be indistinguishable.

At one point, whilst Brenda was still making the journey with me, she became friendly with a girl called Jane, who had come to live in one of the caravans up beyond Rodborough Fort. As soon as she saw Jane on our way to school, she would run to join her, and the two of them would walk on the opposite side of the road from me, and would either ignore me or cast derisory looks in my direction. This sparked a major fit of jealousy on my part.

Maybe there was a falling out between Brenda and Jane, or maybe I was able to poison Brenda's mind over the following weekends, but eventually Fortune's Wheel turned. One Saturday, Jane appeared standing on the field wall just above the cottages, presumably hoping for someone to play with, and I was able to enlist Brenda's support in hurling insults and gibes at her. She soon wilted under our onslaught and ran off back up the Common in tears. Some days later a lady approached me when I was on the Common and asked if I was the little boy who was teasing and being nasty to her daughter. She asked me not to be, since Jane "Really feels it". I felt a modicum of guilt, but we didn't see Jane again. I had won Brenda back!

From the bottom of Rodborough Hill the route to school led along the Bath Road into Stroud, over the derelict and stagnant Stroudwater Canal, then over a rather wide and daunting zebra crossing to the old Stroud Brewery (beloved of my great-grandmother and still emitting a glorious smell of hops). The pavement then mounted an incline passing under the main railway line to London. There were advertising hoardings beside the bridge – some merely promoting rail travel (was it really only 22s 6d for an adult return to London?), some of a more general nature. One exhorted me (and everyone else) to "Go to Work on an Egg", which, for the most part, we did.

Once past the railway bridge, there was Lloyds Bank on the left and George Holloway's statue on the right. He must have set up Holloway's Factory in the nineteenth century, but was best known for establishing the Holloway Original Benefit Society, in which my father and many others invested to supplement sick pay, should it be necessary. Old George's statue pointed a finger at passers-by, though in a far more nonchalant way than Lord Kitchener. My father one day reported that the ultimate indignity had been imposed by someone who had hung a yo-yo on this protuberance.

Generally, we would turn right after the statue and walk up Russell Street, past the entrance to the railway station and the post office on the right till we arrived at Sim's Clock, which stood on a small island in the midst of the traffic, and had been erected the month my mother had been born. We then crossed to Frederick Street, which contained the attractions of Bateman's Toy Shop and Fowler's Cake Shop. In retrospect, it's surprising to think we never entered either at that time of the day. There again, we had to be punctual for school, and in any case my pocket money cannot have been more than one shilling a week, so I at least probably assumed it was more profitably spent on bubble gum and sweets (fruit gums and pastilles, Spangles, sherbet and gobstoppers), at the much cheaper Backhouses Joke Shop at the top of Nelson Street after school or at lunchtime. (It was unheard of for children to bring food into school from Fowler's or anywhere else, or indeed pre-packed lunches. They had school dinner or went home, and the doling out of sweets, which had happened at the infant school, was simply not part of the Church Street regime! We had never heard of the idea of a tuck shop.)

Just beyond Backhouses on the corner of Acre Street was another local institution which I would visit, though only occasionally and always after school, rather than on my way there: Chopper Watts' Barber's Shop. Chopper Watts was of my grandfather's generation and did one style, which was shaved back and sides, short on top: the Chopper Watts Special, which both my father and I sported in the early 60s. In fact, there is a photograph of my father at Portland Bill complete with Chopper Watts Special and a certain amount of excess weight, which makes him look rather like a Mohican. Before Chopper Watts, I had frequented another barber's on the High Street, but both I (and my father) had had to stop going there after I had regaled the barber and everyone else in the shop (including my mother) with the fact that my father had hairs around his willy.

Reverting to my route to school in the mornings, Frederick Street with its toy shop and cake shop joined the High Street, which probably had the steepest incline of any high street in the country. This would bring us in no time to the junction with Church Street, where my female companions (Brenda, Janice and Mary), if any there were, would leave me and proceed on up Nelson Street, past the large Cooperative Stores on the left and Bishop's Junk shop on the right until they reached Castle Street Girls' School – also known as the Blackboy, due to the rather incongruous small statue of a black boy on the front of the main building. This was the junior school my own mother had attended. Backhouses and Chopper Watts' were close by.

Church Street itself was narrow and at first quite dingy, as it ran between high buildings. Though the width of the road itself remained the same, its character changed within about 30 yards, as space appeared on either side. On the left, was the Parish Churchyard and St Laurence's Church itself, which was the church which Aunty Gert attended. On the right, buildings had been cleared to leave an area for car parking. Just behind the church there were some attractive and rather ancient looking houses (where the road turned to the right), and then some more run-down cottages on the right, just before Ryeleaze Road, which went uphill at a steep incline, and on to which the school gate opened.

From that point on Church Street became Brick Row, as it descended past Holloway's Factory to join with Lansdown. (Indeed, the school had been known as Brick Row in my Uncle Maurice's time there thirty years before). However, it was clear that at some point the educational authorities had decided it was better to associate the school with a church than with either bricks or industry and it had changed its name. The school uniform, such as it was (a black blazer and a cap only), had a badge showing a church spire and the words "Aspire High", plus the letters "CSBS" (Church Street Boys' School), all in gold.

The route described was more or less reversed when I went home for lunch on Mondays and Wednesdays, but going home after school was a different matter. In the first place, a conveniently timed bus service was available from the recently opened Stroud Bus Station in the Merrywalks, at the very lowest level of the town. To catch the bus, I generally followed Church Street, not to its junction with the High Street, but making a slight detour to the right under the archway into The Shambles (one of the oldest parts of the town centre, though I was oblivious to that at the time), which connected the High Street to the main entrance to the Parish Church. As you went under the archway, you passed a malodorous gents' urinal on the right and on the left a men's clothes shop, facing on to the Shambles itself. There was a small window in the side wall, which displayed images of modelled men's underwear, and by this I became fascinated and amused.

Having joined the High Street, I would follow it down to the bobby-controlled crossroads, where High Street linked with King Street, Lansdown and, ascending from the bottom of the valley, Gloucester Street. Access to the bus station was via a lane on the left of Gloucester Street and then a flight of steps down to the large area occupied by a covered waiting area and a large space where the buses manoeuvred and parked. To the right was a row of modern buildings, including a cafe, administrative offices and (eventually) an indoor waiting room. Immediately to the left of the stairs was another public convenience. (Stroud was well provided for in those days. Yet a further set (also modern) was situated just to the rear of the Subscription Rooms.)

Some random associations with the bus station:

On one occasion my father stopped on the steps down to the station to speak to Laurie Lee, whom he knew vaguely. (I was aware who he was, because my father had bought a copy of "Cider with Rosie", which had been signed by the author).

One Sunday, when I was there with my parents and sister on our way back from one of our trips out, I thrust my foot into an area of fresh cement, much to my parents' disgust, but possibly leaving my most indelible impression on the Stroud Valleys.

A third memory is of my mother pointing out a particular bus conductress, and telling me that after the War, young women in Stroud still used to send knitted wear (such as socks) to American servicemen who had previously been stationed in the area. So impressed was one of them with the garments received that he asked the girl who had produced them to fly to the US to marry him. (This had been reported in the local press.) When she had arrived, he had taken one look at her and sent her back, and she had ended up working on the buses, for ever after to be the subject of knowing looks and snide comments.

On school days, if Michael Toft had accompanied me to the station, I would leave him at the stop for the Brimscombe bus and go to the far end of the rank of bus stops to wait for the No 429 to Rodborough. The bus was a single-decker and always crowded. It would leave the bus station, run along the Merrywalks past the building in which Aunty Joan Taylor worked, and would then take the Bath Road to Rodborough Hill, up which it would begin to labour. It would not, however, simply mount the hill all the way up to The Pike, but near the Co-op would turn left along Kings Road, where there was a bus stop, and would then run up Coronation Road to turn right at the top into Queen's Road, which was the terminus and where I dismounted in order to climb back up to Rock Cottages, in time for a bread and jam tea. Memory has me listening to "Mrs Dale's Diary" every day over tea, though I am sure I could not have been home by 4.15 when it was broadcast every afternoon.

CHAPTER 14

My second and third years at Church Street Boys' School were something of an educational disaster. Not that I was unsuccessful according to the school's own standards: I always did well in exams and was near the top of the form. However, for various reasons, the actual education which we received was poor, and, in fact, when my family left Stroud and went to live in Gloucester in 1963, it was quite obvious that by the standards of my new school (Lower Tuffley Junior School) I was about two years behind where I should have been, particularly with regard to arithmetic, writing and spelling.

The form master for Standard 2 was Geoffrey Raymond. I liked him: he was fun. He was a great enthusiast for amateur dramatics and a leading light of a community group at Cranham. In consequence, he liked to play act in the classroom, for instance imitating the slouching posture of pupils he wished to ridicule for laziness. He also flattered my precocity, referring to me as "our little Mozart", having seen me with my father attending a concert by the London Mozart Players under Harry Blech in the Parish Church. (Apparently, I had beaten time noisily on the pew.) He drove a Morris Traveller (the half-timbered car), which was always parked opposite the school on Ryeleaze Road and which in those days was very fashionable. He seemed a good teacher to me, but on one occasion Joner burst into the classroom and took him to task for the standard of our arithmetic tests. In front of a classroom of nine-year-olds, he shouted: "I do not like your teaching methods, Mr Raymond" and stormed out!

When it came to our third year at the school, the master who normally took the third-year students (Mr Bartlett) was away probably due to illness, but whatever the reason, my whole cohort had to stay with Mr Raymond and be joined by about a dozen boys from the year below us. The rest of their year stayed with Mr Campbell and that year's new intake. We were therefore in a very large form, and one not only of mixed ability, but of different ages. Although I and my immediate contemporaries would go to Mr Rhys-Jones for a couple of lessons a week to learn "penmanship" (that is, classic copperplate writing executed with a metal nibbed wooden pen dipped in an inkpot), the rest of our education must have been of dubious quality. Further disruption ensued when part way through the year Mr Bartlett returned to the school, took over our form, and, as far as we could ascertain, Mr Raymond found alternative employment!

During those two years lessons in history, geography, nature study, arithmetic, and English trundled on. Geography lessons (aided by a schools broadcast) featured the life experience of boys of our own age – but living in Italy or China or wherever. History lessons concerned King John and Magna Carta, Henry III and Simon de Montfort, and Edward Longshanks, suggesting the then usual concentration on the emergence of the English constitution and empire. (Somewhere along the line we had backtracked from Tar Macadam and the eighteenth century.) One major innovation in our curriculum was letter writing, from which we learned how to lay out a letter and address an envelope. For our cultural improvement we sang together with William Appleby as before.

There was also sport of a kind. The school possessed no gym, so PT was done in the school yard and consisted of races of various kinds, exercises (sometimes involving wooden frames, which I found terrifying), and rounders matches. One morning at play time I was standing by the corrugated iron fence along the Holloway's boundary when I bent down and caught the seat of my shorts on a jagged screw. This caused a major rip. When in the following PT lesson we were divided into teams to race from one end of the playground to the other, I tried to hold my shorts together as I ran. I was destined to fail in this, and, as I raced back down the playground to the finishing line, the whole form, plus Mr Raymond, were bellowing with laughter.

Sometimes – probably on Thursday afternoons – we would be marched in twos all through the town, via the Parish Church gardens and then Gloucester Street to Stratford Park, in which were playing fields for public use. There we would play "touch rugby", though I recall no rules or shape to what we were doing. In Winter, there may have been physical exercises in the school hall, where certainly no gym equipment had been installed, but where a wireless set was on occasions brought in, and this must have been for the purpose of following exercise routines, singing always being confined to our classroom. Once the wireless must have been tuned to the wrong station, for what came out of it was the theme music for "Music While You Work", which every child knew from his earliest years. There was much raucous joining in!

A sports day was held annually. It was actually a sports evening during the Summer Term, and it was held at a private sportsground between Stratford Park and the Gannicox Estate. It was an event to which parents were invited, where rosettes for 1st, 2nd and 3rd places in races were awarded, and at which Joner controlled the proceedings using a megaphone. The only sports on display were running, three-legged races, sack races, wheelbarrow races, and egg and spoon races. My first attempt at three-legged racing (with a boy called Robert Wiltshire) was an abject failure, but the following year Michael Toft and I went into training beforehand, and when our age-group was called we actually managed a yellow rosette for third place, only to have the result disallowed, since someone had cheated. When the race was re-run, however, we received the blue rosette as runners-up!

The issue of school dinners came to the fore in the Autumn Term of my second year at Church Street, and it was then that my mother instituted the new routine of alternating lunches at Rock Cottages and my grandmother's, with a trip to the Skinners' on Fridays. At some point, probably during the Autumn term of the third year, it was suggested in addition that maybe instead of walking/running all the way back to Rodborough at lunchtime, I could take sandwiches and eat them in the Parish Gardens. This was something in which Michael Toft could join too, and, since he was no fonder of school meals than I was, he leaped at the opportunity. For a couple of weeks all went well, until a third classmate, Peter Dyson, asked if he could also accompany us.

Peter had arrived in our class at the end of the first year, was very bright, very Yorkshire, and quite a live wire. He used to address me as "Whah-ti". Maybe his parents were particularly pushy, but they had early on ingratiated themselves with the Rhys-Joneses and socialised with them. The Headmaster's wife gave Peter private lessons, either in elocution or piano, which were her two specialisms, or maybe even in both. He was, let us say, well connected.

The addition of Peter to our previously sedate luncheon routine was fatal, and it was only attempted once! After attracting disapproving glances and "tut, tuts" from other users of the gardens, as we devoured our sandwiches with noise, hilarity and the throwing of food, we proceeded to Bateman's Toy Shop, where we ran up and down the stairs until the manager ordered us to leave. We then espied the public weighing machine outside Boots on the High Street and all three of us mounted it at the same time. This did not pass unremarked or unreported.

When we returned to school, performed our "Atten-TION"s and left-right-left-righted our way back towards our classroom, Joner was outside his office watching the column of marching boys with particular interest. Within a few minutes, a summons was received for White and Toft to attend the Headmaster in the senior classroom, and immediately we were accused of having run amok in the town. I would like to think it was because of my insight into subsisting power relationships, but it was more likely because I was a snitch, but I immediately implicated Peter Dyson as well and was sent to bring him to face a reckoning too. Intended or not, it was a masterstroke, and we were dismissed, not with a caning, of which Joner was a notorious exponent, but with a mere dressing –down, and the (to me) incredible statement that there was no need at all to resort to sandwiches when there were perfectly good meals available on the premises! My father reported a few days later that he had seen repairs being carried out to the Boots weighing machine.

Peter Dyson was one of the boys next to whom I sat during my second and third years. We enjoyed each other's company to such an extent that periodically we had to be separated and made to sit with someone else. It was great fun to stick pencils up the legs of each other's shorts, and before long Peter had amended the wording of the then current hit, "Messing About on the River" by Josh MacCrae, as follows:

"When the weather is fine,
You'll know it's a sign
White's messing about up my trousers!"

Much less fun was to be had when for two lengthy periods I found myself sitting next to a boy called John Wager – the very John Wager next to whom I had been confined during my stay in hospital - who decided to become my tormentor and would try continually to get me into trouble. He smelled strongly of urine, which was hardly surprising in an age when people generally did not wash very much. I probably smelled a bit myself, for in our family we bathed only once a week (on a Sunday), and otherwise I submitted only to a brief wash at the bathroom basin every morning. John lived "at the top of the town", and probably had no access even to those facilities.

Finally, for a brief period, one of the younger intake into Standard 3 was placed next to me. This was Gerry Stewart, who I think lived in Butterow. We got on well enough, but I clearly asserted my authority as an older person: Gerry used to call me Uncle Martin!

CHAPTER 15

Apart from Sports Day, there was little in the school year which stood out from the routine of lessons. There were no extra-curricular activities, such as recorder groups or chess clubs, and the only relief from the humdrum was when occasionally someone would come to give a talk to the whole school about something they either were or had done. In my final year at Church Street a young man called Don White came to tell us of his travels around the world on an initial budget of £26. The encouraging title of the book he had written to tell his story was "Get Up and Go". Our shared surname and the fact I kept his autograph in an envelope for many years kept that title clear in my mind.

There were, however, two more major events in the calendar which helped to distinguish one year from another: Speech Day and the annual School Journey. Speech Day was held in November and took place in the school canteen, so that parents could partake of biliously coloured refreshments afterwards. I attended four Speech Days, and after my first year received a book prize on each occasion – two books on boys' hobbies, and "Ben Hur", none of which I ever read. My final attendance was during the Autumn after I had left the school, when I travelled back on the bus from Gloucester, having been granted special leave from my new school, to receive an award for penmanship. In view of the quality of my writing at that time, the teachers at my new school regarded this award with ironic disbelief.

The three school journeys in which I was involved were all, by modern standards, of modest ambition. At the very first Speech Day I attended Mr Rhys-Jones told the parents that, having taken the school to London the year before, there was no way he would ever consider such an enterprise again, so stressful had been the experience. The restrictions imposed by the limited means of most of the pupils' parents (they had to defray the cost of school journeys) therefore combined with a personal aversion on the part of the Headmaster to ensure that we did not travel far. Certainly, it was never within the realms of possibility that foreign travel would be on the agenda, but neither would it have been on the agenda of any other state junior school at the time.

When the June of my first year at Church Street came around, our journey was focused on the North Cotswolds. We started at Chedworth Roman Villa and ended up in Stratford-upon-Avon, where we visited Shakespeare's Birthplace. Beforehand the school had organised a sort of written quiz for which we had to discover relevant answers at home. How my parents struggled to find the names of the various rivers descending from the Cotswold escarpment both eastwards and westwards!

At the end of the second year, we visited Avebury Stone Circles, where, as Michael and I walked along an ancient embankment, Joner materialised from the mist and asked me to identify the cows which were grazing there. In response to my mumbled ignorance, he took pleasure in informing me they were Frisians. We then proceeded to the sorting office at Swindon Post Office, though I remember absolutely nothing about it! Like all school journeys, this one involved a cheap meal featuring chips and batter, and on this occasion I felt particularly unwell afterwards, as we sat in a local park.

In my final year, we were all taken by train to the Black Country to visit Dudley Zoo and Castle. On the train we were split up between the old eight-seat compartments into which carriages were then divided, and were for the most part unsupervised. There was glorious bedlam when we went through tunnels and all the lights went out! The Castle and Zoo themselves proved an ideal place for boys of our age to visit, with a variety of zoological and historical features to look at and explore (even if the fish and chip meal again turned my stomach). Furthermore, there was a small funfair where we made very good use of the dodgems. The castle was a ruin, if an extensive one. At one point I was challenged by Peter Dyson to accompany him up a narrow winding staircase – something which I declined to do. In our respective accounts of the day, which we had to write up during the following week, he revealed to the world that I had been too cowardly to go up, whereas I claimed that I was concerned it might be too crowded and had intended to go up later! (We know this to be true, because nearly 60 years later we compared notes!)

The journey to Dudley was notable for another reason. Sound asleep in the small hours of the following morning, I was awakened by my mother, who took me into my parents' bedroom and stood me on the front window seat. In the darkness we looked out over Stroud to where a glow suggested a large fire. My mother told me it must be the Ritz Cinema, and that my father had gone down into the town to see what was happening. Still half in a dream, I told her that they shouldn't put things like that in children's books and went back to bed. The following day revealed that the fire was indeed reality, and that the Ritz – one of Stroud's landmarks – was now just a smoking ruin. It was never to reopen.

There had been two cinemas in Stroud: the Ritz just off King Street and the Gaumont near Sims' Clock. I had been taken to both throughout my childhood, though had often had to leave the cinema before the end of whatever film was showing, as a result of nausea, maybe due to eye strain from watching the film itself, maybe due to the smoky atmosphere which blighted all cinemas in those days. Among the films I was taken to see (more often at the Gaumont than at the Ritz) were "Bambi", "Old Yeller" (which terrified me and made me have nightmares about rabies), "Seven Brides for Seven Brothers", "Kismet", various "Zorro" films, "Third Man on the Mountain", and later a double bill of "The Road to Hong Kong" and "Son of Paleface". I also saw a wildlife film which featured dung beetles; but I was asked to sit down and be quiet when I later tried to explain to Miss Bowering's class what dung in fact was.

In the early 60s there were occasions when I was allowed to go to the cinema with Roger, unaccompanied by any adult. "Whistle Down the Wind" was one which we saw together, and it made a particular impression on me, due to its haunting score and bleak subject. When Roger and I went to see "Around the World in Eighty Days", neither we nor our parents had realised how long a film it was. Consequently, we were very late home, and so my mother had another cause to be "frantic". Roger and I were met as we struggled up Rodborough Hill by my father, who had been despatched to find us.

Cinema was not the only formal entertainment to which I was exposed. Apart from the London Mozart Players (at the Parish Church), I was taken by my father to several other concerts at the Subscription Rooms, including one by the Amadeus String Quartet, which I enjoyed

(except for their rendering of a Benjamin Britten quartet, at which I grimaced so much that one of the quartet members winked at me!)

Then there were the shows which were much more my mother's passion. Very early on I was taken to a pantomime with both my parents and Aunty Joan Taylor at the Everyman in Cheltenham. The show itself made no impression, but due to the orange juice I was given beforehand I puked up on the bus home all over my father's lap. When we arrived in Stroud, he chose to walk home to Rodborough. We passed him in the No 429 as he ascended our hill. Through the mud-bespattered windows of the bus, he looked very disgruntled. Others I attended were at the Regal in Gloucester, where the Gloucester Operatic and Dramatic Society (GODS) performed Rogers and Hammerstein, and where an annual professional pantomime was staged. There I saw Michael Holliday and Lita Rosa, whose respective hits "The Story of My Life" and "How Much is That Doggie in the Window" were amongst my favourites. When we went to Bournemouth for our holiday in 1962, we went to see a variety show starring David Nixon, the magician, and the singer, Joan Regan. It seemed the last word in sophistication.

There were a few outdoor entertainments I attended during the Rodborough years. On one occasion only I was taken to Fromehall Park (on the further side of the Bath Road) to see a rugby match in which my Uncle Maurice was playing. In fact, he played for Stroud regularly. Then, as later, the Stroud team was good, but not in the top-flight. My parents one day drew my attention to a national newspaper report on a match involving Stroud (and presumably one of their more prestigious rivals) in which Maurice was mentioned. Nevertheless, my uncle's achievement did not inspire me to try harder at Church Street Boys' "touch rugby"!

Then there was the annual circus (usually "Jimmy Chipperfield's", taking place somewhere in the Cainscross area), and the Stroud Show and Carnival, both in the Summer. The circus and the animals I would certainly enjoy, though I was less sure about the show. However, there was increasingly an element of family pride about the latter, and again it was due to Uncle Maurice, and to the soon to be "Aunty Marion".

Both won a succession of prizes in the photographic competitions forming part of it.

The Stroud Show tents were always pitched on the very fields which saw my non-achievements at "touch rugby", and they in turn were close to Stratford Park. An extremely pleasant afternoon could in fact be spent in the wooded section of the park itself, and this was something I did especially in Summer with my mother, sister, and Roger and Brenda. There was the heady smell of pine, a lake with frogs and newts, and winding pathways to be explored. There was also an entirely separate facility, which we would visit as a family from time to time, and that was the Stroud Outdoor Swimming Pool, or, as I later discovered it was known, the Stroud Lido. This was an uncovered, unheated pool (and kiddies' pool), which must have been built sometime in the '30s. It was one of Stroud's chief attractions to anyone living in the wider area. My father was an enthusiastic, and very good swimmer. He used to tell stories of swimming in the Stroudwater Canal when he was a boy (before the days of the Lido), and the wonderful swimming to be had off the coast of Palestine, whilst he was there during the War. He was keen that in due course Ros and I would learn to swim and made various attempts to initiate us in those icy waters, but without success. Swimming was not something in which my mother would indulge. In fact, I never ever saw her in a bathing costume. She would sit patiently in the sun, looking after the bags, and our clothes (maybe there were no changing rooms) and no doubt worrying about our safety.

CHAPTER 16

Christmases at Church Street Boys' School were given cursory attention by the education authorities. Whereas at the infants' school there had certainly been decorations in the form of paper chains, the Christmas concert, and a party with games and sugary foods, the cheer was more Scrooge-like at Church Street, though we probably did have a tea of sorts in the canteen. Whilst we were under the charge of the drama-loving Mr Raymond, there were additionally preparations for a Christmas play. I cannot imagine what the play was, but it was set on a desert island, and I was cast to play a native – rather than the leading role to which I felt my father's distinction as an actor entitled me. My mother laboured to create a cardboard bone to fit on to my nose and cut up an old blanket to create an approximation of a grass skirt, but on the day of the play I had a cold and did not go to school at all, so my impersonation of a South Sea Islander was lost to posterity.

More generally, impressions of family Christmases are jumbled, for by their very nature the celebrations tended to be repetitive, my mother's family in particular placing great store on maintaining traditions: "That's what we d' always do!"

My mother was a great cake-maker and, in the weeks before Christmas, the mixing, baking, and then decorating of several cakes was a ritual in which I was always involved – helping to lick the mixing bowls clean, and sampling bits of icing and, best of all, marzipan. Again, cards, streamers and holly would deck the living room and hall at 4 Rock Cottages, and we always had a real Christmas tree covered with baubles and trinkets with electric lights and a toy fairy on the top.

Though one or other of my parents would always go to Christmas Mass at Rodborough Church, Christmas Eve was never particularly memorable, since my mother would have been "scaughting" to clean the house and to finish off her cookery. Christmas Day, though, was a joyous event, which would begin with the unpacking of our stockings. My parents would have used a couple of my mother's nylon stockings for this purpose, and these stretched and stretched to accommodate whatever Father Christmas had brought. Unpacking the stockings could therefore be a lengthy process. Not that my parents spent ridiculous sums on presents. They did not have the money or the modern cultural imperative to do so. They went for quantity, rather than luxury, and, along with one major present each year (for example, an Indian costume for me and a crying doll for my sister), they would stuff the stockings with oranges, yo-yos, sugar mice, and small games and novelties.

There would be other presents to open too, apart from those in the stockings. Invariably, Aunty Mue would have sent us six shillings' worth of National Savings Stamps each, an aunt of my father's (whom I had never and was never to meet) called Aunty Mary would have sent money, and another of his aunts, Aunty Faf, who lived in penury in Lincoln, would have sent a few flannels. There would also be presents which had arrived in the post from Dorothy, Brian, and Nancy. (By the time we left Rodborough, there would be a few presents from me to my parents and sister, since I had started buying little gifts out of my pocket money. A bottle of hand cream for 1s 10d was the measure of what I could afford.)

After the ceremony of the stockings and after breakfast, my sister and I would play with our new acquisitions, whilst the Christmas Dinner was prepared. This was always chicken (a meat we ate at no other time in the year), which my parents at least would wash down with Asti Spumante: a drink dear to my father's heart since he had invaded Italy! Occasionally, my Aunty Alice would join us for the meal, which, given my mother's antipathy towards her, must have added a frisson to the occasion of which we children were unaware! One year Aunty Alice turned up with presents for us which were bear-shaped hot-water bottles. We duly received these in the kitchen and thanked her, then retired to the living room to play with our more amusing toys. Somehow one of the hot-water bottles found its way on to the kitchen floor. The Alice frisson was immediately provided: "So, this is what they think of my presents!" she complained in a fortissimo aside. As my mother later told me, this obliged her, whilst struggling with her basting and her duchess potatoes, to assure Aunty Alice through gritted teeth of our very real and undying gratitude.

On Christmas Day afternoon we would go to my grandparents' for a party which could last well into the small hours of 26th. (I can only assume Uncle Maurice ferried us to and from Rodborough.) Those present, apart from ourselves and Maurice, would include the great aunts, Gert and Mue; Mue's son, Lewis; Aunty Joan Taylor (at least for the latter part of the festivities, after her parents had gone to bed); and Alice herself, on whom my grandmother occasionally took pity (even if she was from the other side of the family), if she was going to be on her own on Christmas Evening. Early on, Great-Great-Aunt Kate would also appear, though she would sit for the most part silent in the corner by the grate.

There would be further present-opening upon our arrival, as the various Teal relatives exchanged gifts with each other. My grandmother would have to be prevailed upon to unwrap whatever had been given her, because she tended to sit with her presents on her lap, as if bemused, commenting on the loveliness of the wrapping paper.

My grandparents' sitting room was tiny, but we would all manage to sit round the dining table, firstly for a massive tea of cakes (some provided by my mother), tinned fruit, jelly, and bread and butter. (My grandmother adored Hovis bread spread thickly with butter.) The Teals' table manners were a bit basic. Aunty Gert, who sat hunched almost below the level of the table, would send out an amazingly long arm to grab whatever she wanted. Lewis would also help himself, saying something along the lines of: "Let's try one of these buggers."

After tea and washing up, there might be an interlude, whilst the women talked and the men went "over the boozer" for a pint or two (possible even on Christmas Day!) When they returned, bottle after bottle of spirits would be produced, along with chocolates, sweets, Turkish Delight, walnuts, peanuts, Brazil nuts, and especially Newberry Fruits. Games of Newmarket and Housey Housey (the precursor to Bingo) would be played, with Aunty Gert complaining that nobody was "consecrating" on the game. At about 10 pm, however, the women would begin to serve the Christmas Supper – something entirely unnecessary after the Christmas Tea and our Christmas Dinner, and yet it was tradition. Supper comprised plates piled high with ham and tongue, accompanied by more bread and butter, and lavish supplies of pickles (Piccalilli, pickled onions, Branston, and Red Cabbage). If it had not commenced earlier in the evening, supper would give way to singing, though nothing more complicated than "The Bear Went Over the Mountain". Apparently, "in the old days" Mue's husband, Perce, had been the life and soul on such occasions and had sung songs whilst accompanying himself by "playing the door". I did see his son, Lewis, emulate him once, but by my time it was no longer a regular feature.

Of course, that was the Christmas Day party roughly as it had been planned by my grandparents or as had been hallowed by time immemorial. Variety and additional spice would be provided by family arguments, especially as between the two sisters, Gert and Mue. One of the most spectacular was at Christmas 1961 and its context was a car accident Uncle Maurice had had about six weeks earlier. (Following the break-up of their relationship, he and his former fiancée, Joy, had divided up their engagement presents, and he had been driving back from Gloucester with his share in a thick fog when someone else ran into him head-on. He had sustained only minor injury, but the other driver had ended up in hospital and the cars had been written-off.) Aunty Gert declared that she could never ride in a car with Maurice again, so, of course, Aunty Mue stood up for her nephew as an excellent driver. My grandmother joined in, but was soon reduced to tears. I think the men must have gone over the boozer again or have been (most unusually) in the front room. I went into the kitchen to get away from the fray, but eventually could endure no more, so marched back into the living room and shouted:

"Why don't you all just shut up!", to which the immediate and crushing response from Aunty Mue was "And don't you be a rude little boy!"

Whilst we lived at Rodborough there were no regular Christmas Eve or Boxing Day parties as such, though at the end of 1962 the Skinner Family came to us on Boxing Day with their four children (and another inside Aunty Joan's tummy). My father disappeared at one point and then turned up dressed as Father Christmas, completely convincing the youngest child, Julie, who looked on in complete wonderment. When the Skinners left, it had begun snowing. We waved them off as they started their descent of Rodborough Hill, and the great Winter of 1963 began. There was one other notable Christmas occasion at 4 Rock Cottages, maybe a few days later at the end of 1962, when Maurice and Marion, and possibly our grandparents were present, and at least four of us played Cluedo, and the game simply went on, and on, and on all evening – no doubt to the disgruntlement of anyone else in the room!

Another Teal Christmas tradition was in my experience unique. This was the holding of two "Christmas Pudding Parties" – one at my grandparents' house, just after Christmas, and then one at Aunty Mue's a few days later. A large tea was, of course, served on both occasions, but beforehand the objective was to taste (and express approval of) the hosts' Christmas puddings, which had been prepared weeks before by hours of boiling in the copper (or clothes boiler). Once the sampling was complete (I did not participate), the party would proceed much as it had on Christmas Day, though with less energy and possibly more argument. On one such occasion at Aunty Mue's she managed to work herself into such a state over something Aunty Gert had said that she shook with rage before addressing the gas-lit room with the conclusion that "I don't believe you people d' want to come 'ere!"

She was right: we didn't, and after we had moved to Gloucester, we never did again!

Apart from Christmas, the only annual religious festival of any note was Easter, remarkable not only for the chocolate eggs my sister and I received, but also for my father's tradition of painting faces on our boiled eggs – something he did with considerable skill. Equally, Easter was typified by walks along Rodborough Lane in chilly Spring sunshine, often making forays up the adjoining flanks of the Common to hunt out violets and primroses which grew in abundance.

A final annual event which brought much of the family together was November 5th. This would be celebrated at 4 Rock Cottages with the Teals, Aunty Joan Taylor and Aunty Alice in attendance. All guests would bring fireworks to supplement those already purchased by my parents, and so it would take quite some time for them all to be illuminated or exploded as appropriate. On one of the earliest such occasions the fireworks were set off right by the side of No 4, and unfortunately a rocket was launched at such an angle that it ricocheted down the narrow passageway between No 4 and Rock View. This so terrified me that I ran indoors and hid under the eiderdown on my parents' bed for the rest of the evening! In later years fireworks were ignited down on our garden, well away from the houses, thus avoiding further such mishaps.

Later also it became traditional for there to be an actual bonfire on which a Guy would be burned. He would be prepared by my father, using old clothes, hay stuffing, a mask and various items from his make-up chest. His creations were very effective, though we never had the cheek that many children had to sit our Guy on the street pavement with cries of "Penny for the Guy! Penny for the Guy!"

My mother's contribution was always to provide food for afterwards: usually piles of hot dogs and baked potatoes, though on one occasion she was even more ambitious in preparing a "fireworks tea" beforehand for Ros and myself, comprising various cakes in bilious shades of icing to represent Catherine wheels, snowstorms, and jumping jacks in flagrante delicto.

CHAPTER 17

We moved away from Rodborough on 7 July 1963, and went to live in Gloucester.

The previous twelve months were momentous — and not least because of the weather! The Autumn Half-Term holiday at the end of October had brought an early fall of snow. It did not linger, but was surprising in itself and also a sign of things to come. In the November there was one day a very thick fog — "Killer Smog", said the headline in "The Daily Mail", and comparisons were made with the smogs earlier in the century, already regarded as a thing of the past. That evening my mother and I walked from Horns Road down to the bus station after a piano lesson and could hardly see the streetlamps at all. Then on Boxing Day the Great Freeze of 1963 began.

From that point until at least late February there was continual snow on the ground, and, particularly in early January, deep snow which piled up in drifts. In time this became compacted, and thick ice on the pavements became a ubiquitous hazard. On the first day of the Spring Term, I walked to school by my usual route, seeing far more adults than usual following the same roads, some with chains wrapped around their boots, for cars could in no way cope with Rodborough Hill and there were no buses. Before too many days a modified bus service had been restored, but the severe weather continued and was marked by my mother knitting me a balaclava helmet and buying me my first ever pairs of long trousers.

At Church Street Boys' School there were the inevitable snowball fights. More unusual was the day when, after a slight thaw, a boy in the year above me had the idea of building Venice out of slush and snow near the flat area opposite the main doorway of the school, on which normally we were not allowed to walk. Soon many of us were joining in, turning snow into buildings and bridges, whilst the snowmelt served to create the canals. That a boy from the school should know anything about Venice at first hand was remarkable, and the invention demonstrated so impressed Mr Rhys-Jones that he summoned the local press and secured a photograph on the front page of the Stroud News and Journal.

In the midst of the snowy weather my Aunty Alice moved house from 25 Lansdown to Rodborough, in fact to 5 Field Road, which was part of an old terrace with a garden sloping down towards the Spillmans. It had a dogleg of an access along a completely unmade-up roadway, which connected to Rodborough Hill just below the Prince Albert. At lunchtime, I stood outside the pub watching the removal men negotiating the snow and slush as they transported Aunty Alice's possessions from their van parked on Rodborough Hill along that lane and down to her new home. Not that I was frequenting the pub, but, until the hill became passable, it was there that a temporary bus terminus was located (in place of Queen's Road), so that the bus could take advantage of the gentler slope of Walkley Hill down to the Bath Road and from there into Stroud.

It may have been during the months which followed, or it may have been during the previous Autumn that my father had had the unenviable task of clearing 50 years of the White Family's accumulated junk from 25 Lansdown. (I was never told, and I certainly never even wondered, quite how the estate of the grandfather I never knew, Arthur Wilfrid White, had been divided up: whether the property belonged entirely to Alice and its sale, together with the £832 she had won on a Spastics' Society lottery, financed her purchase of 5 Field Road, or whether it was shared with one or more of her siblings. Whatever the situation, the task of clearance fell mainly to my father.) On one occasion he took me to the property when he was clearing old papers and belongings – including a First World War uniform - and for the most part burning them in the garden. He told me he had found several unexploded hand grenades from one or other of the world wars. At first, he tried jettisoning them in the Stroudwater Canal. Later caution prevailed, and he surrendered them at the police station.

Within a few months Aunty Alice was well settled at Field Road and one Sunday we went to tea with her. She hadn't yet had the opportunity of making the house absolutely reek of tobacco and cat pee, so it was quite a pleasant occasion. On "Pick of the Pops" we heard Gerry and the Pacemakers and the Springfields. By then the snows had passed.

More than anything else, the Winter of 1963 accounted for our subsequent move to Gloucester. My father had by this time been working at "The Gloucester Citizen" for several years, and, of course, had to travel to and from Gloucester every working day by bus. This was a gruelling experience for him in the snow, necessitating even earlier starts than usual and often resulting in his late arrival home in the evening. (His usual bus was having to go via Stonehouse, rather than negotiate Horsepools Hill.) My parents decided that they would not risk this ever happening again, and so in the Spring started house-hunting on the North (Hucclecote) and South (Tuffley) sides of Gloucester. Eventually, they became very interested in a semi at 18 Epney Road, Lower Tuffley, which, by chance was owned by another member of the printing trade (Frank Powicke), whom my father had known through one of his previous jobs. In the early Summer my mother took Ros and myself on the bus over to Gloucester, so that we could meet my father, then visit the house and be shown round by Frank and his wife, who were both very friendly (and keen to sell) and who plied us with drinks and cakes. The house was called "Perpetua": further homage to the printing trade.

On our way by bus into Gloucester that day, we passed the extraordinary sight of the small plane which had crashed into the roof of a house in Tuffley Avenue some days before.

My parents were to purchase 18 Epney Road for £2250, but had first to sell 4 Rock Cottages, which ultimately they achieved for a sale price of £1750. I was more or less aware of the various stages of the transaction: the evening when the estate agent called to talk to my dad and to arrange a valuation, the appearance of the "for sale" board outside, the visits by potential purchasers (though this usually happened when I was at school), including one from and Italian woman who had made no prior appointment and who was sent packing by mother on the basis that "we owe it to the neighbours". Before a sale was agreed, of course, the news had to be broken to those very neighbours. One evening the four of us trooped round to the Gardiners and then to the Heavens. Both seemed genuinely grief-stricken, and as we left the Gardiners' house, Ros ran over to a tearful Edie to be hugged and kissed.

At school I was undergoing the most disrupted of my years at Church Street. To add to the complications of two classes being merged into one, and the gradual easing out of Geoffrey Raymond, one term began without Mr Raymond or Mr Bartlett, or indeed anyone else in charge, for Mr Raymond had had a car crash whilst abroad with his family and was rumoured to have been injured. A supply teacher, Mrs Ritchings (the mother of one of my infant school friends), took over for a few weeks. When eventually Mr Raymond was due back, Peter Dyson, Michael Toft and I lurked in front of the school's main door before 9am, looking through the keyhole to see if we could catch a glimpse of not only him, but whatever injuries he was still sporting. It was Peter who managed to spot him and reported that he was no different: "As like a crested grebe as ever!"

During the Autumn Term a major innovation was made by the school's entry into a poetry recitation festival, which was held at the Subscription Rooms. This was not an event where individuals performed, but one where large groups of children would recite poetry in unison before an audience of parents. Mrs Rhys-Jones coached us for weeks to deliver "Off the Ground" by Walter de la Mare and "The Little Dog's Day" by Rupert Brooke.

I returned on an individual and more overtly competitive basis to the Subscription Rooms not long before I left Church Street. This was for the purpose of taking my Grade II piano examination, for which Jimmy Goodman had coached me. I acquitted myself adequately in my playing, but found the aural part of the exam a bit beyond me. However, I scraped through.

1962/3 was a year when my grandfather had a period of illness – he developed a lung infection, then pleurisy and then ended up in hospital. This was most unusual. He was by that date more than 70 years old, and yet still worked. He had hardly had a day's illness in his entire working life, but he had always been a smoker and at last his lungs were telling him to desist. When I came to Horns Road for lunch one day, we could hear him coughing away in bed upstairs.

"I shall begin to think 'tis all over with 'n," my grandmother said.

But he did recover, and he did give up smoking, exchanging tobacco for peanuts as his habitual indulgence! For ever afterwards there were bowls of peanuts on the shelf over the television, since both my grandparents became addicted!

A more dramatic incidence of illness during the year occurred in the November. I was on my way back to school after Friday lunch at Joan Skinner's when I saw an ambulance parked outside the main entrance to Holloway's Factory. I dawdled for a few minutes before returning for lessons, but long enough to overhear a conversation between two women: "'tis Gertie Teal," one of them said, and then I saw my great-aunt being borne out on a stretcher. This, of course, I reported to my mother, who, when my grandparents were ferried over by Uncle Maurice next morning to deliver "bad news", was able to say: "We know, it's Aunty Gert, isn't it?"

My grandmother (to use her own phrase) looked "shitten" to have her thunder thus stolen, but went on to explain that Aunty Gert had fallen down the steps at the factory entrance and had broken her leg. (Gertie herself later told us that she knew it was a bad break, because she could see the bone sticking through!!) She was now in Gloucester City General, where she remained for several weeks. Ros and I were taken to see her one Saturday, being smuggled in through a French window not far from her bed, since visits by children to a geriatric ward were forbidden. She returned to Middle Street, but before long the Council had arranged for her to be moved to a modern flat over at Mathews Way, Paganhill, where she flourished for the best part of another ten years.

She settled in well and quickly, and in fact kept her flat neat and tidy – so unlike her house at Middle Street – and even became adept at raising house plants. She soon made friends with another resident of the block of flats, though Gert's concept of "friendship" requires some qualification. The object of her attentions was none other than Joan

Taylor's own Aunty Ada Long. Gert reported one of their conversations: "'er met I outside, and 'er turned round and said: 'If you be a-goin' to Stro-ud, will y' get me some S'natogen?' ('er d' say S'natogen, 'cause 'er can't say Sanatogen!), and I turned round and I said: "No, I wun't! No, I wun't!""

Gert never again went back to Holloway's, but continued attending the Parish Church till she died.

My own health at this time was generally good, though it must have been in this year that I contracted German Measles. I received treatment for flat feet (involving having to have my insteps supported by modifications to the soles of my shoes). I also had my first ever encounter with a dentist, other than those who delivered routine check-ups at school. It must have been the Whitsun when I suddenly had a toothache: something more painful than I had ever experienced. My parents dosed me with aspirins and, after the holiday weekend was over, my mother took me to her dentist, Bob Owen, in Lansdown. I was full of apprehension and had to wait outside the surgery breathing fresh air and counting to 1000, but when I was finally in Bob's chair, I was so nervous that Bob had to allow me to hold the forceps myself, whilst he endeavoured to guide the direction in which they were wrenching away at my tooth!

It may not have been 1962/3, (but possibly the year before), but death itself had also impinged on our young lives. I had not been aware at all of the passing of great-great-Aunt Mabel in the late 50s, but early in the 60s a death occurred in my father's family which made more of an impression. My father had an elderly cousin (how many times removed, I do not know). His name was George Dawson. He had worked in the family firm of John White the Printer, and he lived with his wife, Laura, at Cashes Green, not far from Stratford Park. We used to visit them once a year: a journey on foot from Rodborough, which meant going under a viaduct, up what was known as Murder Lane (because the wages clerk of one of the mills had been murdered there), and crossing the railway line further up – all of which engendered some dread. George and Laura were themselves kindly people and they gave us toys, even though we were only distantly related and saw them so rarely. Even then, there was something slightly unnerving about visiting them, because George had been in the First World War, and my father told me he had "trench feet" – though I never witnessed them. Laura, who was small and bird-like, developed cancer and wasted away further. We knew she could not survive long, and one Saturday afternoon, when yet again I was in bed due to illness, I heard the doorknocker and then voices, which I could identify as not only my mother, but George and Laura's son, Paul. Once he had gone, Ros ran up to tell me that "Aunty Laura had gone home to Jesus", so I was a little blasé when my mother came up to tell me the news, and said: "It's ok. I know, already."

"But," my mother said, "it's worse than you think. Aunty Laura died in the night. Uncle George found her, and the shock killed him too!" – something which Ros had not been told at all.

If I remember so much about 1962-3, it is not down to my having kept a diary. I had been given small Lett's diaries once or twice at Christmas, but recorded little other than salutations, such as "Happy Birthday, J. S. Bach" and "Happy Birthday, Beethoven"! Rather it is simply because it was a very memorable and, especially to a ten-year-old, significant twelve months. The move of house above all cemented specific dates and periods in my mind, but there was a surrounding spider's web of other events and developments which all seemed to connect and added colour and association: the winter, politics (of which I was becoming more and more aware in the era of Profumo and the demise of the Tory government), and then there were the Beatles and the explosion of beat music and the Liverpool Sound. It was one of those years!

CHAPTER 18

There were two holidays in our final twelve months at Rodborough – one, comparatively late in the previous year to Bournemouth; the other, comparatively early in 1963 and once more to Swaffham in Norfolk. The latter was as enjoyable as had been previous trips to stay with my uncle and aunt, and left even more impressions.

There was the day which, in Swaffham, was warm and sunny, but which, when we arrived in Hunstanton, was cold and grey under a North Sea fret. We could do no more than go from cafe to cafe, alternating this with trips to play the machines in the amusement arcade: something at which Ros was extraordinarily good, though she could hardly reach the slot of each machine to insert her stake. As we shivered our way along the cheerless streets of Hunstanton, I was able to pick up from other holidaymakers' transistor radios (it was the custom at the time to carry them around at full blast) that "From Me to You" by the Beatles was still No 1. When we returned to Swaffham, Aunty Dorothy beamed and asked: "Did you have a nice time?"

"No, it was horrible," I droned in reply.

Ros and I thought that exchange was so hilarious that we re-enacted it for months afterwards.

It was also the week when my mother received a letter from my grandmother to say that Joan Taylor's mother (Mrs Martin) had died. There was also much on the wireless about political matters. Even at ten years of age, I realised that something important was going on with the repeated news bulletins mentioning the names of Profumo, Keeler and MacMillan.

It was another, and far more domestic incident, however, which most distinguished the week. Aunty Dorothy always served a good tea, and there would often be chocolate marshmallows. From someone (probably Peter Dyson!) I had gained the habit of picking up a marshmallow, whirling it through the air in my clasped hand, and then smashing it against my forehead before devouring it: something which adults seemed to find annoying, but which again I thought hilarious.

On this occasion, I missed out the smashing stage and simply whirled and devoured in one gulp. It was too much for Aunty Dorothy: "I don't think there was any need of that," she spat.

"Oh, Martin!" exclaimed my mother ashen faced, before the rest of the meal passed in all but total silence.

Afterwards I ran up to my bedroom and buried myself in a "Famous Five" book, although I could hear the rest of my family go out of the house with Uncle Brian, leaving Aunty Dorothy herself taking a cello lesson. Anger and resentment gave way to shame and anguish, for I had never been scolded by my aunt before. Indeed, she had been more than understanding over my declaration concerning the "turd behind that hedge" several years before! Eventually, I plucked up enough courage to go downstairs and show my face. Aunty Dorothy asked me to wait until she had finished her lesson, then became her normal friendly self again and took me to meet up with the rest of the family, who were walking near Swaffham Church. I don't think I ever performed the marshmallow ritual again.

The history of that year's transgressions had several other manifestations, which gave the whole period a sense of dislocation and unease. In the Autumn of 1962, there was the small matter of the riot run by Peter Dyson, Michael Toft and myself around Stroud one lunch-time. That October also saw a major mishap at my grandmother's house. I had been taken there by Uncle Maurice, so that I could help him pick apples from my grandparents' one fruit tree. This meant that I picked up apples which he dropped from the branches above – once he had ascertained I was not the sort of boy who climbed trees! In an idle moment, I picked up an apple and aimed it at the fence to the garden next-door. Such was the power of the throw, but the inaccuracy of my aim, that the apple not only missed that fence and the fence to the next house, but went on to smash into the glass panel of that house's back door! I had broken Mrs Wager's window! My grandmother, who had been out at the time, was horrified when she learned of this, and I was distraught with guilt, though fortunately Mrs Wager was very forgiving. It is strange how the mind works: that weekend stays with me in surprising detail. In the first place, the Saturday was the 13th of the month, and, though not a Friday, I had told myself something awful was bound to happen. In the second, it was a weekend when Uncle Maurice took us out for a day-long trip on the Sunday. We went to the Brecon Beacons, and on the way back stopped at an Italian cafe for food. Both my uncle and I thought the place stank of feet. Only much later did I realise we had smelled Parmesan cheese. The date, the apple and the cheese were then forever linked. It was a madeleine moment!

At school I came near to another scolding from Joner, when a boy in the year above me started teasing me. Having escaped from him one afternoon after school, I ran from the premises at such speed that at the bottom of the rather steep Ryeleaze Road I could not slow down sufficiently to avoid running straight into Church Street. I was lucky that the only traffic coming my way was an older boy on a bike, but he had to fall off his bike to stop hitting me.

"You little fool!" said the school caretaker, who happened to be passing, but who, it seems, did not know my name. Sure enough, in assembly next morning, the incident was recounted by Mr Rhys-Jones as an example of someone's colossal stupidity, but I remained unidentified – and silent. Shortly afterwards my dad (who must have been having his weekly day off) came to meet me from school, so that he could speak to the bully and take him to task. This he did, but later said it had been embarrassing, since the offender was a mere shrimp of a lad!

A further dramatic (to a ten-year-old) event occurred on my 10th birthday, when I had a party to which Michael Toft, Peter Dyson, and (by way of reciprocity) Gerry Brown were invited. We left school, ran down to the bus station and mounted the No 429. We were very boisterous and soon attracted the ire of Miss James – the old lady who had given out sweets so regularly when I was at infant school, and who had always previously regarded me with benign approval. We were told off and indeed she reported me to my father when she next bumped into him. Worse was to come over tea. My mother was single-handed and struggling to keep order between four ten-year-olds. At one point Peter Dyson and Gerry Brown pursued each other round the table and Gerry knocked a bowl forming part of my mother's only tea set on to the floor where it broke. My mother was remarkably restrained and only hissed the words: "We'll see what my husband has to say about that when he comes home!"

However, seeing myself as the champion of authority, I told Gerry Brown, when we started playing formal party games, that he would have to pay for the dish. At this the hard man of Standard 3, the naughtiest boy in our year, dissolved into tears and would participate in nothing further that evening. When my father came home and took over the running of the games, my mother, to her credit, took Gerry into the kitchen, sat him on the table and talked to him about his life and his interests for an hour or more, before escorting him all the way down to Stroud bus station to catch his bus back to the top of the town. "Your mum's smashing," he told me the next day, and she was.

My parents' preparations for the move to Gloucester occupied much of the Summer. My father had ordered a batch of tea chests, which were duly used for packing, and a couple of which were used by me to create dens in the garden. In those last few weeks, however, I was more preoccupied with school and exams, but also with another mishap which almost ruined our departure. Once again, Brenda played an important role!

From time to time, I picked up words and expressions from others, which I eventually discovered were frowned on by my parents. Later I was told that they had resolved never to swear in front of myself and Ros, and this they stuck to throughout our childhood. The worst my father would come out with was "Stone the Crows", whilst my mother might say "Damn, sod, blast, and set sail to it!", if frustrated. One afternoon at Church Street some boys approached me and asked (as I thought I heard it) if I had a kent. When I said I thought so, they went into screams of laughter, then explained it was a girl's "thing". When I enquired, my mother told me it was a very bad word, which I must not use. It was from Brenda that I picked up another less vulgar, but in the event devastatingly rude expression: "old cow", as applied to an older woman.

A few weeks before we left Rodborough, Jimmy Chipperfield's Circus came to town as usual. We were due to go as a family, and I knew that Roger was hoping his mother would take him and Brenda too. It was not to be, and I overheard a very upset Roger being told he could not go. Maybe my parents assumed it was something to do with Mrs Heaven and said so in front of us, but the next morning on our way to school I asked Brenda why her "old cow" hadn't let Roger go to the circus. I thought no more about her reply, whatever it was. The White Family attended the circus on a Friday evening, and my sister and I had a wonderful time, especially when we were given cardboard clown masks to take home with us. The next morning, we donned them and ran out to play. I should have realised something was wrong, because, when we approached Roger and Brenda, Roger said: "We're not talking to the likes of you," and they turned on their heels.

Oblivious to impending doom, Ros and I ran across the paved area in front of Rock View. As we went past the kitchen, the door opened, and Stella Heaven called me over: "I hear you called me an old cow, Martin. That's not very nice, is it!"

Horrified behind my gaudy mask, I blurted out the first thing which came into my mind: "Daddy said it!", and then ran away to my parents to confess what had happened.

They were not amused. In fact, they were furious, and my mother immediately went round to Stella to apologise and to tell her that it was absolutely untrue that her husband had said such a thing. The apology was accepted, but I was later told that it had been the nearest I had ever come to a "jolly good hiding". For two long weeks I could not forgive Brenda for repeating what I had said – particularly because I knew that I had picked up the offending expression from her. I refused to play with her, even when she and Ros were playing together. Eventually, though, with time running out before our departure (as my mother pointed out to me) I had to clear the air, and I asked if I could join in; a request which was conceded, at first with ill grace, but for the last few days things were almost, though not entirely, back to normal.

On our last morning, we said farewell to Roger and Brenda and the Gardies. No particular emotion was expressed, any more than it was to be when I left Church Street for the last time two weeks later. Mr Rhys-Jones shook my hand and more or less complained that I was leaving - "Just when we thought you would do some good for the school's reputation", as if it was my fault!

At ten years old, it is not easy to envisage what life will be like without those who have been your friends until then. Perhaps I imagined that, once we had moved house and had settled down in Gloucester, we would make regular visits back to Rodborough and would keep in touch. As I later learned, though, children have a remarkable ability to compartmentalise: to move on from friendships when their environment changes, and not look back. That realisation was in the future. For the time being, it was enough to say goodbye and see you soon to Roger, Brenda and the Gardiners. For some reason, I was reluctant to say goodbye to Mrs Heaven – maybe I was still smarting with guilt at what I had said a couple of weeks previously. However, my mother prevailed on me to go round on my own, and Mrs Heaven and I just looked at each other until Stella broke down in tears and I mumbled a "goodbye" and left.

When Pickfords had packed their van with our possessions, my father sat next to the driver with Stumpy on his lap. Once they had left, Ros and I went with our mother down to the bus stop in what seemed like an unsettling dream, caught the No 429 to the bus station, and then the Gloucester bus to The Fox and Elm: a ten-minute walk from the next chapter of our lives.

CHAPTER 19

Little of that first weekend in Gloucester remains with me. The new house was in chaos with tea chests everywhere waiting to be unpacked, as my father struggled to produce some order. No doubt my mother helped at the outset, but before long she went down with a migraine – as she was prone to at moments of stress. This would happen at the start or finish of a holiday, and for many years she would often have a migraine or what she called "a bilious attack" or "one of my heads" on a Monday, no doubt due to the stresses and strains of the family weekend!

My parents' bed had been made up in the largest of the house's three bedrooms, and that was where my mother retired for most of the Saturday and Sunday – soon joined by Stumpy, who had had her paws buttered to encourage her to spend time licking them and, in doing so, to become accustomed to her new environment! Whether the butter was in any way useful or not, Stumpy decided that the gap under my parents' bed was the safest place in her altered universe, and that is where she stayed for several days.

There were three bedrooms on the first floor. The largest was my parents' room and was at the front of the house. It soon contained the utility furniture which had occupied their room at Rodborough, but now crammed into a much smaller area. Behind that was a smaller room, which looked out over the main garden, and contained an airing cupboard and emersion heater (which was vastly more efficient than the old Ascot). The room had the added attraction (to me) of golden stars stuck all over the ceiling. This became my bedroom. There was then a little box room at the side of my parents' room, which had two outer walls and was consequently cold and damp-feeling, and this was allocated to my sister. My father had made the mistake of asking both myself and Ros which bedroom we would like, and both of us had said "the room with the stars". Fortunately for me, age and possibly gender triumphed and we were not forced to draw lots or flip a coin.

The only other room on the first floor was a bathroom, which was again smaller than the one at Rodborough. It had a toilet, bath and basin, all in very close proximity, and a window through which in the distance you could just glimpse the Malvern Hills to the North-West. There was a small landing on to which all of these rooms opened, and above it a trapdoor giving access to a loft. In the nineteen years of my parents' ownership of 18 Epney Road I never once ventured into the loft, and indeed the only person who ever did was my father, who, typically, would not bother with a stepladder, but would balance on the top of the banisters, from which he would open the trap-door and then swing himself up into the space above. This was not something he needed to do often, for little was stored up there. The only occasion when he spent more than a few minutes in the loft occurred a couple of years later when there was an unusually heavy snowfall in early March driven horizontally by a south-westerly gale. Next morning I was woken by the dripping of water on to my face from what turned out to be a snow-filled attic. That evening my father had to spend several hours up there filling buckets with the snow which had blown in under the rafters and between the tiles.

The ground floor of the house was similarly compact. You climbed a large step to enter the front door (beside the sign saying "Perpetua" in blue lettering) and found yourself in a short hallway with the staircase rising a few feet in front of you on the right. Immediately to your right was a cupboard for coats and muddles, and to your left two doors leading to the two living rooms. The one at the front of the house (decorated by our predecessors in alternate panels of yellow and dark green wallpaper) housed the piano and at first the dining room table and chairs. The slightly larger room at the back was where the settee, armchairs and tv were placed, though within a few months my parents had reversed this arrangement, and the back room became and remained the dining and main room, whereas the front room was "for best" – an echo of my grandparents' house. Both rooms had a grate which was operational, coal being kept in a metal bunker just outside the back of the house. The rear living room had a decor which my parents found embarrassing: the two large alcoves either side of the fireplace having wallpaper of a brightly coloured and modernistic design suggestive of a '60s coffee bar. Within a year this had yielded to my father's first redecoration project: the boarding up of the fireplace (in favour of an electric fire), the papering of all walls in a lightly patterned green, and a general repainting.

There was also a kitchen, the door to which was directly ahead of you as you entered the house. It was very small, perhaps only half the size of the Rodborough kitchen. It had fitted cupboards and a tiny pantry under the stairs, in front of which there was just about enough room for the cooker and the Flatly clothes dryer, as well as a basin, with cupboards beneath and a draining board. The only working surfaces were provided by the cupboards adjoining the sink, plus the tops of the refrigerator, the twin-tub washing machine (another new purchase) and a small free-standing cupboard, all placed on the left of the kitchen underneath some of the fitted cupboards. This was the space in which my mother had to do her cooking and baking as well as the laundry and, to be frank, it was a bit of a hellhole in which she had ample scope (and reason) to become fraught and on occasions manic, particularly when she was preparing Sunday lunch, or, most alarming of all, Christmas lunch!

At the front of the house was a squarish lawn with flower borders, and an empty flattened area on which Frank Powicke had parked his car. The boundary with the road was marked by a low red brick wall (the whole house was of red brick) and an evergreen hedge. The garden at the back of the house was much bigger. After a small concreted area, which was quite a sun-trap and later much favoured by my mother for working up her annual tan, there was a lawn, further flower-beds, a trellis and rose arch, and behind that the vegetable garden, which had a sizeable conference pear tree and several apple trees. On the right was a large green wooden shed, which Frank Powicke had used for printing (which seemed to be an all-consuming hobby for him, as well as being his profession). We used it for muddles and toys. Behind the shed was a greenhouse, which became a passion for my mother, since she was able to raise flowers from seed to populate the various flower beds, and later to grow tomato plants. A slightly elevated concrete path ran down the centre of the garden to the back fence and gate. Either side of it the soil was very different to the black loam of Rodborough. It was compacted clay which, as my parents were to find, was back-breakingly difficult to dig.

The house was a semi, probably built post Second World War, and was in a short road where all the houses were semis of the same design. In fact, several of the nearby roads all followed the same pattern, though

Epney Road had fewer mature trees along the roadside than was true of them. If you looked at our building from the roadway, our half was on the right, the other half being owned by a family called the Morehens: a married couple with an infant daughter called Julie. As far as I know, during the next nineteen years until they left the area, my parents never went into the Morehens' house, and the Morehens never came into ours. We were on friendly speaking terms, and in due course my father would strike up more of a relationship with the husband, Dave, after my father finally bought a car (in 1968) and was able to obtain tips about maintenance. Dave's hobby was in fact his car and his motorbike, care of which occupied so much of his time that I rarely remember him taking the car out on to the road! His wife, Doreen, was pleasant, but very quiet and shy.

As with most sets of semis, we had far more to do with the family who owned the left-hand side of the next house down and with whom we shared a fairly wide concreted access (with no gate, when we first moved in). These were the Martins: an elderly couple, Jim and Beatrice May, and their youngest son, Malcolm, who lived there with his own wife, Dorothy, and their infant son, Kenny. The younger family moved out after a year or so to their own house – an identical semi in a road about half a mile away. The parents remained: Jim until he died in 1969, Beatrice May until she died only shortly before my parents themselves moved away in 1982.

We became firm friends with Jim, who had a serious heart condition and was often ill. His passions were football and horse racing, neither of which was approved of by his wife, who was a strict Baptist. In due course, Jim would come round to spend Saturday afternoons with us, so that he could watch "Grandstand" for the horse racing and the football results and could check his Zetters pools coupon. (He would tell Beatrice May that he had come round to watch "Danger Man"). Jim had an account at one of the local book makers and was always well in surplus. It financed little treats and presents for his wife, who had declared that if she found out that Father had been gambling again, or if she found any of the proceeds, she would buy a hat with it!

Beatrice May did not endear herself to my mother, not only because of the way she treated Jim, but also because of her many prejudices, not least of which was her conviction that any bad weather was inevitably the fault of "the spacemen". She was also a bit of a snob, having worked in service many years before, and referred to "the superior sort of person", not because she considered herself one of them, but because they were owed deference. Despite the tension these idiosyncrasies created, when she became ill at the end of her life, it was often my mother who visited her and ran errands, whilst no one from the Baptist Church went near her.

When we first moved in the rear of our property was separated from the shared access by a high grey-painted fence with trellis along the top. This ran from the corner of our building (by the back door) to the corner of the green wooden shed. A beautiful and luxurious yellow/pink rose bush grew in front, until a couple of years later a high wind blew the fence down and caused the rose bush to be cut off at the roots. The grey fence was then replaced by a larch-lap fence, but later, when my father started using the shed to house a car, that fence was relocated towards the house, making the "garage" more functionally part of the driveway.

At the rear of the Epney Road semis was a very large field used for sports purposes associated with the Lower Tuffley Community Centre, a rather decrepit and possibly asbestos-containing building to one side of the field. During the Winter, goal posts would be erected for local football matches, with one set quite close to our own back fence. For the rest of the year the pitch was unused, and in a small way compensated Ros and me for our loss of the fields and Common at Rodborough. Wildflowers flourished in the grass, which itself grew quite long in the Summer. When mowed, the drying grass provided ample scope for games which involved building haystacks and burying ourselves in them. We would also go into the field to play with the Martins' dog, Judy, a young and very gentle Alsatian. Stumpy established an easy dominance over Judy, but was traumatised one day when Judy's much larger and more aggressive brother, Sabre, visited the property and did not take kindly to Stumpy's attempt to scratch his nose under the gate.

From the front of 18 Epney Road you could observe the other "compensation" for our loss of greenery. Rising above the red-brick semis and flowering cherry trees of Nympsfield Road was the quite imposing sight of Robinswood Hill. Without knowing its name, we had been aware of this outlier from the Cotswolds for several years. It was quite prominent on your right as you approached Gloucester on the Rail Car. It could also be glimpsed from vantage points on the Western edge of the Cotswolds, such as Frocester Beacon. It had a conical shape, was about 650 feet high, and had a lot of tree cover. Several years later, when my sister was doing a school project for which she had chosen Robinswood Hill as her subject, we discovered old pictures of the hill during the seventeenth century when it had been virtually denuded of all vegetation, presumably because it had all been used for firewood by the nearby city. By the 1960s, however, patches of woodland had re-established themselves – except in one area: the quarry – a great yellow gash in the side of the hill, which could be seen from miles away and which gave the hill much of its character. When we moved to Gloucester, I believe the quarry was still operational, though all activity had ceased before the end of the decade. The hill is now even more wooded, and you cannot identify the quarry from any distance.

During the period between our arrival at Epney Road and the beginning of the next school term we as a family made several forays up the hill to make its acquaintance. All ascents were steep and generally by way of narrow paths overhung with foliage, and so it was very different from Rodborough. Fine views could be had from the summit, where there was a trig-point, but the hill's great disadvantage was that it was not a mere matter of yards from our front door, as had been the Common at Rodborough. Even to begin an ascent, it was necessary to walk along estate roads, or the ring road (Cole Avenue), which ran along the far side of the field, for a distance of at least a mile.

CHAPTER 20

If Epney Road with its uniform houses, small dimensions, and generally dull setting sounds poor exchange for Rock Cottages, this was not something which immediately suggested itself to my ten-year-old mind. Indeed, there were many advantages which it had, and which emerged over the following twelve months. I did not feel particularly sad to have moved to Gloucester. It was simply something which we had to do, because my parents had said it was necessary. I also did not particularly miss my school friends or spending so much time with Roger and Brenda. We had moved, and that was it: I simply made the most of playing in the garden and field, and by this point, of course, Ros was no longer a tiny infant, but was six years old and therefore far more companionable.

If I had a brief instance of melancholic reflection, it was upon the second Sunday of our residence at Epney Road. My mother was cooking dinner in the tiny kitchen, whilst I sat on the sofa, which for the time being at least faced the back window of the house. To the accompaniment of Bobby Vee's "The Night Has a Thousand Eyes", I focused on the pear tree (still a major novelty) and thought about the changes of the previous fortnight, uncertain whether I was happy with them or sad.

There was of course no complete break with our previous social life. My grandparents, Aunty Joan Taylor and Aunty Alice all made visits before many days had passed to see the new house. In due course, Michael Toft was invited over one Saturday and we were taken to the Barton Fair, where the two of us had the alarming experience of going on "The Rotor", which was a revolving cylinder, the walls of which rose and the floor of which fell, whilst those who were on the "ride" appeared to ascend its inner walls by a combination of centrifugal force and a ribbed rubber surface which seemed to stick to their clothes! I also went over to Stroud (on my own), climbed Rodborough Hill and collected Roger and Brenda from Rock View, so that I could accompany them on the bus to Tuffley for their one and only visit. Much later in our first year in Gloucester the Gardies made a visit – having by then forgiven us for leaving Rodborough. Strange to say, the only moment during that visit which stays with me was when, shortly before they left to catch their bus back and we were all watching "Top of the Pops", Edie said, as she watched Colin Blunstone of the Zombies delivering "She's Not There": "Oh, don't he frow-en!"

Even Aunty Mue and Lewis came over to see us. It was the Sunday of the annual Royal Variety Performance, which almost everyone with a television would watch. That year it featured Harry Secombe doing a medley from "Pickwick", but most significantly of all – The Beatles. While John Lennon enjoined the wealthy to rattle their jewellery in time to the music and Paul McCartney paid tribute to Sophie Tucker, Aunty Mue watched fascinated, with her eyes watering from short-sightedness. It was probably the first and last time in her life she watched the Fab Four on screen, and it was the occasion when I watched a money spider spin a web from her mop of grizzled hair to her shoulder.

When we moved to Gloucester there were still two weeks left of the school term, and, whilst it had been decided that my sister would immediately join Lower Tuffley Infants' School, my parents felt it better that I should round off my term at Church Street Boys' before starting the new term at my new junior school. Extra lunches with my grandparents and Joan Skinner made this viable, and I survived the fortnight unscathed. In order to attend school during those two weeks, I had to get up especially early and travel back and forth to Stroud on the bus all on my own. This was something I adjusted to quickly, and the extraordinary thing was that my parents were perfectly content for me to do so, accompanying me as far as the bus stop by the Fox and Elm only on the first day.

At the end of the fortnight there were no sad farewells to anyone –only Joner's rather resentful handshake on my last day at school! Then I crossed the car park on Church Street with Michael Toft, said goodbye to him, and went down to the bus station, simply relieved I would not have to make the journey so frequently in future! As for Michael, I must have been thinking: "Goodbye for now, Michael. Will be seeing you soon!"

And I did, of course, see him again - on the day we visited Barton Fair; but we never again met or wrote to each other after that. Neither do I think I even bade farewell to Peter Dyson, who by then was at least my second-best buddy! Perhaps he was on holiday. (It is ironic that many decades later we rediscovered each other in Birmingham through Facebook and became fast friends again —as if little had intervened, though he had been a horn-player with the CBSO and I had been a partner in a large solicitors' firm, to say nothing of the rest of life!)

Piano lessons continued for a while, and I travelled over on the bus to see Jim Goodman on a Saturday afternoon. At some point in the following Autumn, however, lessons ceased, probably at my mother's initiative, and the piano stood idle in our new front room for the next three years, until first Ros and then I became pupils of Mr Ross Williams, who also taught Beatrice May's granddaughter. In the interim, my interest in pop music burgeoned and a picture of the Beatles on "Juke Box Jury" (taken from "Fab" Magazine) soon adorned the wall over my bed. I still had a degree of guilt about this, and when Aunty Dorothy and Uncle Brian came for their first visit the following Summer and were taken on a tour of the house, I was devastated to realise that I had failed to take the picture of the Beatles down before they went into my bedroom!

My Aunty Nancy came to stay during our first six weeks at Epney Road. The circumstances for this were, however, sadly different from those surrounding visits from other relatives and friends just wishing to see "the new house". Whilst we had been living at Rodborough – perhaps as early as 1961 - it had been explained to me that Nancy's husband, Joe Lampitt (the uncle who had become annoyed with me for not knowing the times of the local bus services), had tried to commit suicide. We had seen him once or twice since then, and, to me at least, he had seemed the same as he always had done, except that he had lost much of the use of his right hand and arm. Apparently, when, following his ingestion of large quantities of barbiturates, he had spent several days in hospital, the nursing staff had failed to notice that he was lying on his right arm and continued to do so for many hours until he suffered nerve damage.

When one afternoon during the two weeks I remained a pupil at Church Street Boys' School I returned to Lower Tuffley, I was surprised to find my Aunty Alice in the front room having tea with my mother. There was an atmosphere, though there often was when my mother and Alice were together. A few minutes after I had joined them, however, my mother said: "Martin, you know what Uncle Joe tried to do before. Well, this time he's done it."

I took this to mean that he had killed himself, but later as I lay on my bed thinking about it, my childish mind could not really accept that it could possibly have happened. Had my mother meant that he was dead, or did she merely mean that he had made another attempt? How was I going to discover which was the case? I could not live with the uncertainty, so marched downstairs to the kitchen and asked outright how Uncle Joe was. My mother looked shocked:

"Didn't you realise, Martin. He's dead," was all she could say.

It emerged that my father had been contacted that morning at work by Nancy herself saying she had lost Joe. My father had gone straight up to Hillingdon on the train to lend moral support, and returned quite late that evening. A week later he went up for the funeral. When he returned on that occasion, it was again very late, but I could hear him reporting matters to my mother: "There was really only one surprise."

"And what was that?"

"Joe's son!"

I learned later that it had only been after she had been married to Joe for several years that Nancy herself had found out that he had been married before. That he also had a son by that marriage she only discovered at the funeral. This was something my parents simply could not credit, though my gentle-natured aunt was always someone to leave well alone and not ask questions – after a youth under the tutelage of Aunty Alice. I also learned that the night before Joe was pronounced dead, Nancy had said to him that she had forgotten to set the alarm clock.

"Never mind," he had replied. "We shan't be needing that in the morning," and despite his previous attempt and presumably signs of depression in the previous few weeks, she didn't think any more about it - until the following morning.

Within a couple of weeks Aunty Nancy had come to stay at Epney Road for a few days. Ros and I were asked to be very careful what we said, but we had no experience of deep bereavement, so we simply behaved as normal, and, to our relief, so did Aunty Nancy. Apart from one instance when my mother said that Aunty Nancy was crying at the words of a song on television, she seemed her usual humorous, scatty, lovable self.

It was the first of fairly regular visits over the next few years. She might stay with Alice at Christmas, but would come to us for a long weekend perhaps a couple of times a year, always apologising for being late or putting us to trouble, but always entertaining us with stories of her own escapades at work or on holiday. (She seemed to have had a riotous time in Cyprus and, for some reason, in Monchengladbach!) She would also tell risqué stories, which were usually lost on me. I could not imagine what was so funny about Marianne Faithful and a Mars Bar.

Her visit continued until the late 60s, when she developed multiple sclerosis (though even then on one occasion she came all the way from Maidstone, to which she had moved, in a taxi to spend two hours with us and then make the return journey). Ten years after Joe's suicide she was dead herself. My mother, who always had a predilection for psychosomatic theories, was convinced this was the result of shock and guilt and never having come to terms with her loss.

CHAPTER 21

The Summer holiday between my leaving Church Street Boys' School and joining Lower Tuffley Juniors was marked by The Great Train Robbery and by the guilty excitement it caused. "She Loves You" was No 1 by the end of August. In the more mundane world of Epney Road, we enjoyed further visits from friends and relatives, became accustomed to playing with Judy in the field, made the occasional trip to Robinswood Hill, and rather more shopping trips to Gloucester by way of the No 9 double decker. (In those days there were no major supermarkets in the town centre, the main attractions being the Bon Marché ("the Bon"), Marks and Spencer, and smaller shops like Currys, Smiths, and the SPCK Book Shop. There were also two cinemas, the Regal at King's Square and the Odeon in Eastgate Street, to which we were taken from time to time.) By late August, however, the novelty and distraction of national news and our new life gave way to frequent attacks of butterfly stomach, as the start of the new school term loomed larger.

Lower Tuffley Junior School was only five minutes' walk from our home. All I had to do to get there was turn right out of the drive, continue to the end of Epney Road, where there was a small roundabout, cross Lower Tuffley Lane (to the right) and take a narrow footpath between gardens to the school playing fields, which were crossed by a pathway leading to the main buildings. The school could also be accessed from another footpath on the opposite side of the fields, which connected with the Infants' School attended by my sister, or through the main gate, which could be reached by going down Lower Tuffley Lane – a road with pre-war redbrick semis on one side and our field on the other - and then taking a short cul-de-sac to the left, almost opposite the Community Centre.

The school was co-educational – something I had not experienced since infant school. It had a school colour, rather than a formal uniform, and this was brown. The girls usually wore a dress of brown and white cheque, though not all did, so it could not have been compulsory. None of the boys wore brown blazers or caps, but what was certain was that boys could only wear short trousers, so the long trousers bought for me during the Winter of 1963 were relegated to the back of the wardrobe. Both sexes were encouraged to wear brown woollen jumpers or jerseys.

The post-WW2 school buildings themselves were single-storey and roughly in the shape of a "T". The top bar of the "T" comprised most of the classrooms, of which there were a fair number, since each of the four years was divided into three streams. It ran parallel to the cul-de-sac with the main gate. The supporting bar of the "T" contained the school hall (which was equipped as a gym and had a stage at one end), a couple of offices, a long corridor beside the hall, and the school canteen at the far end. The main entry to the building was at the intersection of those two bars, where there was an entrance hall, which had the long corridor and the doorway to the hall on its right, and on its left a short passageway leading to the main classroom corridor, but also the headmaster's office.

The headmaster was Mr Alderton, who in personality terms was more than a match for Joner. Physically he was much shorter, had receding ginger hair, a florid complexion and a rasping Yorkshire voice and accent. I guessed this was where he came from, because the accent was like Peter Dyson's. He was very strict, very efficient, and ruled the school with both a metaphorical rod of iron and a much more physical rod of bamboo. Despite that, he was very fair, and, though I found him intimidating the first morning when my mother presented me at his office at 9.30, in time I came to respect and almost like him.

After brief introductions, my mother departed and Mr Alderton led me (gently by the ear), not towards the classrooms, but along the corridor next to the hall towards what I could smell was the canteen. It was there that the school's top form (4a) was housed temporarily, whilst additional classroom space was being added beside the canteen on part of the school's rear playground. This meant that the thirty or so members of the form were all seated on benches behind four or five lines of dining tables, three to a table and with their backs to the canteen serving hatches. The pupils faced the teacher's desk with a blackboard on either side. Each child was responsible for keeping his or her writing materials and a few books in brown cardboard boxes which sat on the dining tables in front of them. The whole strangeness of the set-up did not strike me – I accepted it as what it meant to be in

Form 4a! In time, however, before Christmas, the form moved to a newly completed teaching space just beyond the canteen, which was very cramped, but at least contained proper desks and chairs. Finally, in the New Year, another move was made to a thoroughly modern classroom in the new extension, which had bookcases, storage cupboards and a revolving blackboard. The other two streams in the fourth year also moved to the extension at the same time.

Our form master was Mr Bolton, who would then have been in his forties, seemed tall – certainly taller than Mr Alderton, had thick horn-rimmed glasses and greased slicked back hair. He in fact lived very close to us: a few doors up Nympsfield Road. He was quite intense and very well organised, but almost always overwhelmingly jovial. He was one of the best teachers I ever encountered in any context.

That first day was nightmarish. I knew no one, apart from a girl in the row in front of me, who was called Sandra Frost, and had to be one of my "girlfriends" at Rodborough Infants' School. At playtime I approached her and asked if she was from Rodborough. She said she was, blushed, and ran off to play with her friends. At lunchtime I went home to eat and then panicked, because I did not know when I was supposed to be back for the afternoon classes. Fortunately, a boy by whom I was sitting in class, a very lanky kid called Neil Symonds, who also lived in Nympsfield Road, passed our drive as we finished eating, and I was able to point him out to my mother, who rushed out to extract the necessary information from him. By the time I returned home at the end of the day I was almost in tears: there was so much which members of Mr Bolton's class had to do, not least homework (which I had never encountered before) and this included an arithmetical "problem" to be solved every day!

What became obvious quickly was that, for all my good exam results and annual prizes, Church Street Boys' School had never stretched me, and yet now I was in a class of comparatively high achievers – the top thirty out of an intake of ninety. I was also way behind them especially in terms of arithmetic. I knew nothing of fractions and decimals, whilst the rest of the class had been dealing with them for a couple of years. Similarly, I had only recently learned "penmanship", whereas my fellow pupils had been doing "joined writing" for most of their time in the school. Though I went back to Church Street to receive a prize for penmanship that term, my new educators considered my style of writing archaic and my neatness non-existent. Finally, there was my spelling, which was rapidly assessed to be poor.

The major focus of Lower Tuffley Junior School was in fact to ensure the maximum number of passes at the 11 plus exam, which we was due to take the following Spring. For that purpose, there was far more concentration on arithmetic and English than had ever been the case at Church Street, and this was at the expense of other subjects, such as history, geography and nature study. I soon grasped that my fellow pupils knew very little of these three topics, and I consistently outperformed them whenever this was put to the test, but that was seldom and, in the general scheme of things, unimportant. What was important was to show mastery of the spelling of a series of lists of words, and the solutions to a series of arithmetical questions. There was even a list of proverbs which we had to learn by rote.

To remedy my spelling, I was put into a special set of the less able pupils, who were regularly drilled and tested by Mr Alderton himself. With regard to arithmetic, I was so far behind that this necessitated personal tuition after school from Mr Bolton, leading to extra homework. As for my writing, the school decided that it was pointless to try to teach me the modern-style script employed by the rest of the form, but it was impressed upon me that I must improve my neatness.

It took several months of considerable effort on my part, hours of homework, help from my parents in testing me on my "lists", but dedication above all from Mr Bolton for me to begin to catch up. When we took exams just before Christmas, I ended up 11th out of the whole form. (We were seated in the order we had achieved in the exams to emphasize the competitive relationship we all had to each other and for us to recognise our nearest rivals!) By the end of the school year I was 3rd, and was in fact 1st of those boys who were progressing to the Crypt Grammar School the following September.

Looking back on the inevitable humiliation I felt at finding myself so far behind in my studies and on the extra work I had to do to catch up, I had no great feelings of injustice or misery – except perhaps for the first couple of days. The totally new situation regarding my schooling, like the loss of my rural environment and my previous friends, was something which, as a ten-year-old, I didn't resent or resist. Maybe this was because it was so much part of my family's, and in particular my mother's attitude to life that you played by the rules, did what you were told, and accepted what authority told you to do. Many years later a friend, who was a psychiatrist and whose idea of an enjoyable evening was to spend it doing IQ and personality tests, exclaimed that someone had done a very good job on me!

CHAPTER 22

Despite its lack of emphasis on history, geography and nature study, Lower Tuffley Junior School held a more rounded attitude to education than had done Church Street. Music, drama and sport all had more clearly defined roles in our curriculum.

Early on in my time there I was urged to take up the recorder, which was what most of the girls and a few of the boys in Mr Bolton's form had already done. This must have coincided with the end of my piano lessons with Jimmy Goodman. It seemed a fairly painless exchange in terms of the effort involved, and would also help to allay any expressions of alarm at the lapse in my musical education emanating from Swaffham! As it happened, I already possessed a recorder, because Aunty Alice had given me one for Christmas a year or two before. Once or twice a week, therefore, I and several others from my form went to Mrs Freeman for tuition. My ability to read one line of music and my early realisation that untidy sliding and slurring could be avoided by judicious "tonguing" of the notes meant that I was soon able to establish some sort of pre-eminence in the group, which helped compensate for my lack of success and self-esteem in most other areas of school activity! That said, we did not progress very far with our recorder playing, and it did not feature much in my routine after the first few months.

I was fortunate (as was my family) that I was not persuaded to take up the violin, which was really the only other option for musical endeavour. The sound of about half a dozen of my classmates playing through a few pieces in the school entrance hall with a teacher (who a few years later was dismissed for improper behaviour with his young charges) was excruciating. One of the tunes still lodges in my mind in all its awfulness.

As at Church Street, we did have some singing lessons, and again it was largely thanks to radio's "Singing Together" with William Appleby. However, those sessions and other singing tuition were not left to Mr Bolton. For those we went to the school hall where Miss Bowen supervised us from the piano. She was a full-time music teacher, in addition to playing piano for the hymns in morning assembly. I once heard Messrs Alderton and Bolton expressing surprise to each other, having just found out that Miss Bowen had in fact been William Appleby's accompanist at one stage.

Of greater significance in terms of the amount of time I devoted to it, and indeed to my life as it later developed, was the emphasis that was placed in Mr Bolton's form (but not in other classes in the school) on drama. Mr Bolton's class was the senior class in the school, and to it fell the task of mounting the annual nativity play. Not that this was a matter of improvisation by the pupils themselves. It was, instead, the result of many weeks of planning and rehearsing organised and run by the headmaster's wife, assisted by Mr Bolton. Mrs Alderton was even more diminutive than her husband, but had a more pleasant disposition. She was not a teacher at the school at that time, but came in specifically for the purposes of rehearsal. (The Aldertons had a daughter, Joy, who was in my form, and who, at the age of 10, was already almost as tall as her mother, though when I met her again about 6 years later, the family's genetic disposition seemed to have reasserted itself!)

For the Christmas of 1963 the Nativity Play was to be "Leap as an Hart" (the grammar of which title was beyond my comprehension). I was cast as First Shepherd, along with Neil Symonds (No 2) and Henry Stinchcombe (No3). We had a scene to ourselves "on the hillside" and then, of course, some lines by the crib. The "action" of the piece was punctuated by carols sung by individual characters or groups of characters. Inevitably, the three shepherds were required to sing "While Shepherds Watched Their Flocks by Night", only, at our first run-through, it became clear that Neil and Henry could do no more than growl and mutter, while I was left singing the tune. To their relief, it was decided that I would sing on my own. However, that was not to be the end of it, because the "production team", then decided that my talents should not be squandered and that I should take over other carols during the piece. Eventually, "The Citizen" drama correspondent (or was it one of the teachers subbing on behalf of the school?) reported that I had had to sing four carols "before the audience would let him go". It seemed to me I had "arrived" – I was at last fulfilling the family tradition, following in my father's dramatic and my mother's vocal footsteps, and putting behind me the disappointment of being cast at Church Street as a non-speaking South Sea Islander!

The favourable reception of the nativity play had consequences later in the year. So flushed was she with her success, that Mrs Alderton decided to enter her most talented actors in the schools' section of the Cheltenham Festival the following Summer – something which had never been undertaken by Lower Tuffley Juniors before. This time I was cast as the Swineherd (who turns out to be a prince in disguise) in "The Princess and the Swineherd", the princess being interpreted by Mrs Alderton's daughter, Joy. Her first line was: "How do I look," as she gazed into a small mirror, though I recall none of my own speeches.

Apart from delivering lines (whatever they were), I had to play a bird-whistle when a fake budgerigar was brought on stage in a cage. The bird-whistle was a curious device consisting of a metal receptacle, which was filled with water and to the top of which was attached a thin metal tube. I had to blow vigorously into this, the bird song being produced by the bubbles I made in the water! It had a rather piercing sound. At the end of the festival drama competition, we felt well satisfied with ourselves (though in retrospect, perhaps we should not have been) when we ended up third equal out of a field of five!

Mrs Alderton's enthusiasm for our theatrical education manifested itself on a third occasion during the year – in fact, several months earlier, in the March, when our whole form was taken to the schools (ie junior schools) performance of Shakespeare's "Richard II" at the Crypt Grammar School. On the afternoon before the performance Mrs Alderton gave a special lesson in which she explained what the play was about (concerning which I must have been irritatingly knowledgeable, due to my immersion in "Age of Kings"). She also impressed on us how eminent Crypt drama was in national terms, due to the presence on the staff of one Charles Lepper, a former professional actor at Stratford. In the event I adored the experience of seeing Shakespeare live. Even if I personally had already been programmed to find it captivating, it was the more surprising that my classmates also seemed to enjoy it. A schools audience of as many as 400 children watched and absorbed a show of about two and a half hours all in blank verse, without being rowdy or disrespectful. It was a different age, of course, but the production was magnificent!

Shakespeare had impinged on the school year right at the start, when I was still in a panic over all the things I, as one of Mr Bolton's pupils, had to undertake, and before I had in any way found my feet in the class. It was probably during my very first week that Mr Bolton announced that we would be producing a class magazine called "All Our Own". Each child in the class was required to submit a contribution. I had no idea what to do, or what would be appropriate, and I made the mistake of asking my father, whose concepts of what children should know about or be interested in had previously been shown to be a little awry - not that I was conscious of this.

"What about 'Shakespeare's Views on Richard III'?" he ventured, and, with my implicit trust in him, I immediately set about drafting what those views might have been. Only, my views on "views" were also a little awry, for what I produced was a family tree of the Yorkists and Lancastrians with a footnote of about two sentences' length. Mr Bolton was visibly non-plussed when I presented it to him, but had the presence of mind to suggest that instead I might pen a little piece about Rodborough, about which I had already been prevailed on to give a five minute talk to the form. In the end, to my surprise, both pieces appeared side by side in the magazine. To be honest, my description of Rodborough was as unimpressive as my "Views", amounting to little more than a hand-drawn sketch of the Common and the location of our old house, the fort, Winstone's and The Bear, but at least it implied that (apart from studying Shakespeare) I had led some normal sort of life before joining the school!

The class magazine was not the end of our literary training. During the third term of the year, after the 11 plus had been taken, each child in Mr Bolton's form had to produce a lengthy written piece of fiction, to the writing of which at least one lesson a week was devoted. Building on my interest triggered by "The Land of the Pharaohs", I produced a tale which revolved around the Nile, mummies, and hidden treasure. Its actual writing was, however, the least of my troubles, for I was appointed as the editor of the collection of youthful tales, which meant that I was responsible for ensuring a neat copy had been obtained from each child, and that it was placed between thick bound board covers. In these I had to punch holes and insert metal eyes through which coloured tags had to be passed and tied together, to ensure the physical integrity of each "novel". This was so that the whole corpus of work would be preserved, could be studied by our successors in the following year's 4a, and could inspire them to even greater creativity. Apart from the fact that the editor's role was a lot of work, the implement I was given with which to fix the eyes to the covers was defective after too many years' use/ misuse, and the results were less satisfactory than I (and Mr Bolton) had hoped. I doubt it mattered, for it was no more likely that the following year's 4a would have any more time to read our efforts than we had had to read those of our predecessors!

One final element in the school's strategy to improve our self-confidence and powers of expression (concepts quite unrecognised at Church Street) was the requirement that each of us in turn had to give a five-minute talk to the rest of the class, a talk being delivered nearly every day. Once we had been round the class the first time, there was then a second round of talks, and then a third. After each talk the class had to vote on marks out of ten, and scores were no doubt then entered on a wall chart. (4a had a lot of wall charts). During the course of the year, I gave talks on Rodborough, East Anglia (assisted with my collection of postcards of Swaffham, Norwich, Kings Lynn and Hunstanton), and Henry V, and I was engaged on preparing a talk on Queen Victoria when the school year came to an end. Because I had based my talk on Henry V entirely upon the text and pictures of the Ladybird book on the monarch, Mr Bolton told me I had been very lucky to score 10 out of 10!

CHAPTER 23

If you looked out of my bedroom window at 18 Epney Road, you saw the garden, community centre field, and Cole Avenue in the foreground, and in the far distance May Hill and to its left the hills of the Forest of Dean. May Hill was a place we had once visited with Uncle Maurice before leaving Rodborough, and I had been disappointed that none of his slides of the occasion showed my Richard III impersonation under the sinister shade of the pine grove crowning its nearly one-thousand-foot peak. Unfortunately, neither May Hill nor the Forest were places we could visit conveniently until my father finally learned to drive and bought a car five years later. We did make one attempt to visit the area by public transport, but it was a dismal failure, when we found that May Hill was a very long way from the bus stop for services to and from Gloucester!

In the middle ground of the view from my window was the Podsmead council housing estate, and beyond that the Gas Works. To reach Podsmead, you turned left from our drive and went to the opposite end of the road from the junior school. In that location was a large, concrete, and very prominent footbridge, which took you over Cole Avenue to the point where the entrance to the Crypt Grammar School was to your right and a large grassed area was straight ahead of you. The grass was surrounded by housing, but there were also a couple of shops (including a post office) and a small police station, and, at the far end, a fenced area with a slide and other pieces of play equipment. During our first few weeks in Gloucester, and before I started at my new school, we visited this occasionally with our mother. Later it was an area we were allowed to go to unaccompanied. Even in those days Podsmead was a bit of a rough area, but not so as to make us feel unsafe, or, more importantly, make our mother imagine we might be unsafe.

Cole Avenue itself was a dismal creation – useful to drivers wishing to avoid the city centre, but, apart from the footbridge, featureless and bleak as it ran from the Bristol Road up past Podsmead and the Crypt on its left, over the railway bridge and up to St Barnabas Church on the Stroud Road. It was separated from surrounding green space by concrete posts and mesh fencing, sometimes adorned with what I later came to realise were used contraceptives. The Council made attempts to mitigate its appearance by planting trees along its verges, but they would frequently be broken off by vandals. It took decades to establish the mature trees which now make the road almost attractive.

It was what lay beyond Cole Avenue, the housing and the playground which gave the area a particular distinction, not to say aroma, namely the Gas Works. It sported huge circular holders, chimneys, gantries and large stockpiles of coal, for this was the era before North Sea Gas and a much older and polluting technology than was associated with that innovation was still employed. In fact, the discharging of clouds of foul-smelling effluent was a feature of the Works, the area and our lives. Those clouds would sweep down over the play area, the housing estate, Epney Road, my school, the Crypt School, and the residential streets further beyond, and this might happen several times in one day. Everyone in the area had been assured that there was no risk to health, and this we accepted, whilst holding our noses!

Similarly, it was a regular feature of life in Epney Road in 1963 and for several years afterwards, that our water supply (which, we understood, came indirectly from the River Severn, rather than from some Welsh reservoir) would become severely discoloured for several hours at a time. It would, in fact, turn a yellowish-brown colour and might even contain sediment. Again, the authorities had said that it was all perfectly safe, and so, in that more trusting age, we accepted this, waited a few hours for our cup of tea, and boiled all water for the rest of the day. It didn't interfere with bathing, of course, because that was so infrequent anyway!

Beyond the Gas Works was the main A38 (the "Bristol Road") and beyond that the Gloucester- Sharpness Canal. One Sunday afternoon our parents did attempt a family outing by foot down to the main road and then back through the grounds surrounding the Gas Works, which were simply wasteland with masses of brambles (and presumably vast amounts of pollutants under the surface), but the attractions of twentieth century industrial architecture remained to be discovered, let alone shared by us, so it was a trip we did not repeat.

It was possible to access a much more attractive stretch of the Canal, if you went down Cole Avenue to the south, and after a brief stretch of the Bristol Road, took a turning right along a secluded residential road, though there was no bridge when you reached the Canal. To cross it, and then follow country lanes down to the Severn itself, you had to go further along the Bristol Road, before turning right. This was, however, quite a long walk there and back – maybe taking up most of a Sunday afternoon. Though I did indeed take that walk on a number of occasions over the next few years, in the whole nineteen years my parents lived at Epney Road I never once bothered to go and see one of the reputed wonders of the area: the Severn Bore.

The other coordinates of our new existence included a parade of shops at Slimbridge Road, which could be reached either by going up Nympsfield Road (opposite our house) or by going along Epney Road to the roundabout near the school and then turning left up Tuffley Lane. For most of our food needs those shops were sufficient, for convenience foods, such as fish fingers and beef burgers, were playing an increasing role in our diet, and my mother could also buy suitable meat there for her stews and shepherd's pies. She would go into Gloucester perhaps once or twice a week to stock up with better produce, perhaps from the old market, where the worms which used often to be seen on trays of fresh fish were not the best of advertisements, but to which, despite my personal distaste, no great exception seemed to be taken by my mother or anyone else. My mother did seem to shop every day – either at Slimbridge Road or in the city centre. More than anything else, this was due to our lack of transport: there was only so much she could carry in her shopping bag, so frequent trips were inevitable. Additionally, food storage space at No 18 was severely limited, and, whilst we had a fridge, no one we knew had a freezer.

Then there was the community centre itself to the side of the field at the back of our house. We did not become active participants in its various activities, except on two occasions. One of the demands placed on members of Mr Bolton's form was that each pupil should attempt to read one book from the school library and one from the local lending library every week. I joined the lending library, which was in the community centre, and soon became an avid reader of Captain W.

E. Johns and G.A. Henty. Later my parents did go along to the inaugural meeting of what was intended to be the Lower Tuffley Community Centre Drama Group, but never went back, pleading "too many commitments", once they'd taken the measure of the other potential members.

However, the real impact of the centre upon our lives made itself felt on Saturdays. There was almost always a dance organised on Saturday night, and loud pop music, both from local groups and via vinyl, would boom out over the field and the surrounding area until perhaps 11pm. This was not something to which I in particular objected. It was rather exciting to hear tracks from the "Please Please Me" LP, such as "I Saw Her Standing There", at full volume quite late in the evening! It spoke of another world which perhaps might (but in the event didn't) await me in a few years' time! The only times when I frequented the community centre in later years were when I helped out with a play group during the summer holidays in the early 70s and when I went to an after-show party for the Crypt's production of "Macbeth" in 1972!

CHAPTER 24

My sex education advanced a step (or rather, several) in the course of my year in Mr Bolton's class, though this was not due to any formal instruction, or as a result of at least fifty per cent of my class being female. Very soon after I joined the form, I became friendly with a boy called Gerry Connor, who lived close to us in one of the older red-brick houses in Lower Tuffley Lane. He came from an Irish family, and his father had died. As the evenings became longer after the New Year, I would often spend time with Gerry practising our roller-skating up and down the pavement of his road. We would also go to Gloucester swimming baths on a Saturday with another boy called Jimmy Bonfield, and would spend hours in the pool until our fingers went wrinkled with the effect of the chlorinated water. It was either on one of those occasions or before a swimming lesson, when all three of us were changing in the same cubicle, that I announced in my usual informative manner that the Queen was pregnant with another baby (the eventual Prince Edward).

"Dirty old woman," said Gerry, whilst Jimmy sniggered. They then revealed to me that, for a woman to become pregnant, her husband had to stick his cock up her arse. After several days rumination on this, I told Gerry that this could not possibly be right. "After all, can you imagine Sir Winston Churchill doing that with Clemmie?"

Gerry could. It took him another few weeks to come up with the further information that one detail of his revelation had been wrong, and that it was not the arse which required penetration – something Jimmy seemed to verify when he explained that the expression "Get knotted" meant get knotted with a girl's whatsit, or so he speculated.

It was also Gerry who passed on the news that girls had something called "periods". He explained that their "parts bled" and that at least one girl in our form was already subject to this. For quite a while I had the disquieting mental image of girls going round with their nascent breasts smeared with blood. I supplemented these snippets of information with sneaked forays into the family's old dictionary to look up rude words. Ultimately, however, I found it all so distasteful and confusing that I resolved to put the whole subject of sex out of my

174

mind and return to my previous state of innocence. This I more or less achieved until I progressed to the grammar school!

The presence of girls in class 4a made for one of the most obvious and major contrasts with Church Street. Though I had remained friendly with Brenda and with Janice and Mary Young whilst I had been a pupil in Stroud, now was the first time for three years that I had been educated with girls. It is difficult to say what difference it actually made. Behaviour in the classroom and the schoolyard was definitely made more civilised by the presence of females, and I remember none of the scraps and aggression which had been typical of the boys only school, though that might have been down to tighter discipline. In the yard the boys seemed content to kick a ball around or simply chat together, whilst the girls were more genteel with their skipping, French skipping (which I also found fascinating), and hoola hoops. The girls also seemed more self-assured and academically successful than the boys, and at the beginning of the year girls occupied most of the prestigious seats starting on the teacher's right – demonstrating their superior results in the previous year's examinations.

Top of the form throughout the year and occupying the No 1 desk was Christine Phelps. She was not only a very bright, but a very determined young lady, and I had not been in the form more than a couple of days when she decided that I was to be her new boyfriend. There followed two weeks of friendly chats at break times and even a trip to her home to meet her mother one Sunday afternoon. However, I was in for a lesson in the female temperament when on a joint trip to the Community Centre library she suddenly announced that she was tired of me, stormed off, and ignored me for most of the remainder of that first term.

By the following Spring the social imperative of pairing off had again asserted itself. A rather plump girl called Mary had decided that I was her intended, and I started to visit her every evening after school over in Podsmead. I even became a regular guest at her parents' council flat, where I went for tea and (to my horror) listened to Jim Reeves records. She was rather more mature than I was and perhaps too mature for her age. She would try to kiss me on occasions – once in the middle of the Cole Avenue footbridge - and it emerged after a while that she was herself subject to periods. When her sister hit her one evening, she had to go home in tears to change, and when she came back announced that her mother thought she was pregnant – for what precise reason I never found out, but I was uneasy with the thought that I might be suspected of having had something to do with it!

I was rather alarmed in general by her attentions and decided to counterbalance them with some further intrigues of my own. I took pity on a girl called Jennifer and occasionally went to her house in the evening too. And then there was Miriam, whom one dark Winter's night I had escorted home from school, which, in my mind, created an additional entanglement and made her my third girlfriend.

Though I felt obliged by society's norms to enter into these imaginary romances, and though in general I got on very well with all of the girls in my class, I was much more comfortable in my friendships with boys. Apart from Gerry Connor, I was particularly friendly with a boy called Philip Horsley, mainly by dint of the fact that he had joined Mr Bolton's class at the same time as me, though he had suffered none of the issues I had done due to my being so far behind with my studies. My other main friend, though, was Timothy Parrott, who came from quite a large family, of which the mother was Chinese. Ying Sha was an amazing woman who sold toffee apples door to door for the church and called me "Marting". One Christmas my mother met her outside the grocery shop at Slimbridge Road. She seemed well in the Christmas spirit, and when she saw the queue at the shop announced that it was "Like a flipping faming!"

By the end of the school year Gerry, Tim and I had become very close, and yet changing schools that Summer altered everything. Tim went with me to the Crypt School, we shared our grammar school and our university education, and have remained in touch, often on a very regular basis, ever since. Gerry went to "the other" grammar school, Sir Thomas Rich's, on the other side of Gloucester, and for no logical reason we completely lost touch. From the time we left Lower Tuffley Junior School on only one occasion did we exchange words, which would have been about a year into our grammar school careers. That day Gerry passed our front drive and we had a difficult and brief conversation making comparisons between the two schools. Once again it seemed that childhood friendships were almost entirely a function of environment. When I left Church Street it was in part understandable that I lost touch with Michael Toft and Roger and Brenda, because they lived ten miles away. Gerry Connor lived just around the corner! Just as odd in retrospect was the fact that, when Tim Parrott and I went on to the same grammar school, we were for one year in different forms, and during that year rarely spoke!

Perhaps the apogee of my social life that year occurred on the occasion of my 11th birthday in March 1964. My parents arranged a party at 18 Epney Road on a Saturday afternoon. Those invited were my three girlfriends, Gerry Connor, Tim Parrott, and Philip Horsley. There was the usual tea, but I remember no games, no sticking tails on a picture of a donkey whilst blind folded, no apple bobbing! Instead, as my parents reported to other relatives and friends: "The children entertained us!"

What transpired was that we decided (and I think it must have been on the girls' initiative) to compose and perform little sketches on humorous topics, which proceeded on a semi-competitive basis. Miriam declined to participate (but at least swelled the audience for our endeavours!) So, it was the three boys against Jennifer and Mary, who, for all that they were rivals for my hand, worked together like a well-rehearsed comedy duo. A year before, my party guests had run amok, and Gerry Brown had ended up in tears. This year we behaved as the paragons of self-confidence and inventiveness which Messrs Bolton and Alderton were striving to create! And yet, a year later I had all but lost touch with Gerry Connor, and Tim I saw rarely. (Philip had moved away from the area.) Though I attended Mary's birthday party the following November we watched the Daleks returning to "Dr Who" and the Beatles first performing "I Wanna Hold Your Hand"), and though I once saw her at a wedding many years later, that was the only contact I ever had with any of the three girls after we had proceeded to grammar school. Single sex education had re-asserted itself.

CHAPTER 25

If school swimming lessons were responsible for advancing my sex education, they had the less important effect of finally teaching me how to swim. My father had been trying to teach me and Ros for several years and, particularly since we had moved to Gloucester, had taken us regularly to the indoor heated baths the city possessed. These were the old Victorian baths in Barton Street, shortly to be replaced by a modern facility (which inexplicably was about two feet short of the length required for it to qualify as a venue for international competition!) It was, however, the fact of weekly swimming lessons with the rest of Mr Bolton's class which finally impelled me to stay afloat without an inflated rubber ring. Maybe this was another aspect of "catching up" with the rest of the form. Within weeks I was also practising seal dives, though I never summoned up enough courage to jump from the diving board itself.

Sport was much more organised than it had been at Church Street, and again I found myself woefully inept and inexperienced compared with my fellow students. During the Winter months there was soccer, which I had never played before and which I hated. Instead of random running about the pitch "tagging" other players to secure the ball in "touch rugby", I found myself being told how to control the ball with the instep of the foot (which seemed perverse – I didn't even know what an instep was before) and to head the ball (which I found frightening). I mastered neither skill.

In the Summer, there was cricket, which again I had never played, though the West Indies v England series of the Summer of 1963 had at least generated in me an enthusiasm for the sport – as long as it was someone else who was playing! Maybe it rained regularly when we were due to play cricket, but my only actual participation in a match was when I was the designated scorer for a fixture against another school – a role at which I was no more skilled than as a player.

A particularly bitter experience occurred early on when some piece of equipment was required for the purpose of soccer practice and I was sent by Mr Bolton to fetch it from the school hall where Mrs Mountford, the form mistress of the fourth year "C" stream, was teaching some gymnastics to the girls of the year. Wishing not to disturb her, I started rooting through various cupboards to find whatever it was Mr Bolton had requested. Mrs Mountford was not amused and shouted at me for my rudeness in not asking her permission to do so when she was in the middle of a lesson. In my panic to do the right thing, I had made the wrong call, which is not difficult when you are ten and out of your depth! I hated and feared her for the rest of the year.

There were other aspects of my education in Mr Bolton's form which were entirely new to me and were hence challenging, if only because they contributed to a feeling that there was never a moment free, and that constant achievement and self-betterment were essential at all times. As well as music, drama, sport and "editing" the novels which we all wrote in the final term, I became the "maximum and minimum" monitor, which meant that I had to supervise a chart showing the maximum and minimum temperatures outside our new classroom, as revealed by a special maximum and minimum thermometer. Furthermore, each day I had to take a different child out to the thermometer, so that they too could learn its intricacies and record the results!

Like all other members of the form, I also had to hunt the press every week for a suitable cutting ("News-sheet") to which to append an explanatory note, all examples of which were then placed on a large notice board curated by a girl called Josephine Hyatt. As with "Shakespeare's Views on Richard III", I tended to hit the wrong note with this activity. Whereas my classmates would rejoice in items of local news from "The Gloucester Citizen", my focus was more on international affairs. Josephine was not impressed when I produced a tiny picture from "The Daily Mail" showing the Sultan of Zanzibar, together with my rather lengthy note explaining that he had been overthrown in a revolution.

Certainly, during the first term of the school year another set of skills the school attempted to impose upon me related to craft – again something which had never been attempted at Church Street. At least twice a week the boys in the class and those from another class were hived off to be taught by a glamorous young teaching assistant called

Miss Kennedy. She was Welsh and had one of those rather rigid bouffant hair-dos popular in the early 60s. (I can only guess that simultaneously the girls were being taught elsewhere something to do with needlework or cookery.) The only items which I produced in the course of these lessons were a work folder in which to put my later efforts (should there be any), and an "animal" constructed out of pipe cleaners around which were wrapped lengths of glued paper, the final result of which was then painted red and green. Miss Kennedy was rather impressed:

"Oh, look at 'is 'hyers!'" she said, and indeed my beast did sport two elephantine protrusions at the sides of its head.

It survived many decades on a succession of bookshelves.

Then in the final term there was French – something which the school (like most other schools in the country) had never before sought to teach to eleven-year-olds. Fortunately, it was a mere taster course for spoken French, with no formal grammar input. It was clearly a challenge for Mr Bolton himself, but he managed to make it fun for us all, and I progressed to grammar school with no aversion to modern languages – in fact, quite the reverse.

Of course, the biggest challenge of the whole year was the 11 Plus Examination, which was held in the early Spring. Having ensured as far as possible by Christmas that those, like me, who were behind with their studies had caught up, the emphasis switched in the following term to regular rehearsals for the exam itself. On at least a weekly basis we sat what were effectively "mock" exams, using old papers for both arithmetic and English. I have no recollection of the contents either of the "mocks" or the real thing, other than that one question required us to write a paragraph about our favourite television programme. I wrote about the "Dick van Dyke Show", though I could equally have written about the "Lucy Show" or "Perry Mason", all three of which were part of our regular viewing.

Then began the long wait until the results arrived in the form of letters to our parents over the Easter holidays. In the event, I had passed for the Crypt School, and this necessitated my father going along to the phone box at the end of Epney Road to telephone the news to Swaffham! In fact, every child in my form had also passed, as had half of that year's "B" stream. Back at Church Street three out of a slightly smaller form passed for grammar school, one for technical college, and the rest all proceeded to the secondary modern. (Such information was always published in the local press, but this set of results was confirmed to me many years later when Peter Dyson re-emerged in my life.)

At the end of the year Mr Bolton would tell us that ours had been a strange year in which either all could have succeeded, or there could have been significant failures. Who knows on what he based this, but in retrospect it is difficult to see how the extreme degree of benevolent cramming and drilling to which we were subjected could have produced anything but the very best of results. Had I remained at Church Street, such an outcome for me as an individual was very far from guaranteed.

CHAPTER 26

The Christmas of 1963 coincided with the initial peak of Beatlemania. Following their appearance on the Royal Variety Performance, increasing mass hysteria at their concerts, the return of "She Loves You" to No 1, and its then replacement by "I Wanna Hold Your Hand", they seemed to be the most important aspect of Britain's national life.

At school, the Annual Concert and Nativity Play were followed swiftly by the end of term Christmas parties, which were organised on a form-by-form basis. Perhaps because of our seniority, but more likely because we had not yet moved into our new classroom, Mr Bolton's class was allowed to use the school hall and in particular the school stage for our festivities. Beatles song after Beatles song was played, and Mr Bolton organised a competition to find the best dancer in the form. In groups of about eight at a time we went up on to the stage and twisted, shook, and gyrated to find out who received the loudest applause from the rest of the form. I know I twisted for all I was worth, but excited no great response. The ever-encouraging Mr Bolton muttered to me that he thought I'd deserved better!

Within the class we were also encouraged to post Christmas cards to our special friends. These were collected in a big cardboard posting box and then distributed on the final afternoon of the term. Mr Bolton told us that he hoped no one would end up without any cards as a result of this process. (He claimed this sorry result had occurred on at least one previous occasion.) To counter this possibility, three of the girls made sure they had sent a card to everyone in the form. Of course, the result was then that one person received just three cards, so that everyone, himself included, realised that he had no close friends.

As for our family Christmas, we must have been collected and brought back by Uncle Maurice for us to attend my grandparents' party. I can only assume that was so, because the following Christmas, when my mother had recently had an operation, we most certainly did not travel over to Stroud, and this was a major departure from a routine which had seemed immutable. On Boxing Day 1963 Aunty Alice and Aunty Nancy (who was staying with her) came over to Gloucester by bus, and we spent much of the evening playing Newmarket and eating peanuts. In fact, I ate so many peanuts that I was violently sick – fortunately after the aunts had left – and was exceedingly unwell all night.

A week later, the most important aspect of the New Year was the advent on the BBC of the first edition of "Top of the Pops". One of the acts featured was new to us: The Rolling Stones, to whom my mother took an immediate dislike. In fact, she was so disgusted with them that she wrote to Robert Robinson on tv's "Points of View".

"What a way to begin the New Year," she wrote, before going on to describe what she'd seen – "And singing, of all things: "I Wanna Be Your MAN"!!"

Her letter was not read out, and she came to regret her hasty judgement. Strangely, it was Aunty Alice who first became an avid Stones fan – until she read that they'd been caught pissing against a wall, which she considered scandalous. (Aunty Alice would also be way ahead of us in her later enthusiasm for Sonny and Cher!)

Apart from the festive season, there were, as far as my family was concerned, several other significant events which coincided with our first year in Gloucester. On my father's side, we were of course still coming to terms with Uncle Joe's suicide. On my mother's, it was the prospect of the wedding of Maurice and Marion the following June which occupied most of our attention. Their engagement had been a low-profile affair the previous Summer, with no big party or celebration. It only became clear to my mother that they were engaged when the couple treated us to a day on the Glamorgan Coast, and, as they took it in turns to drive, she espied that both were wearing rings! They admitted their news at the first coffee stop!

The wedding itself took place at Holy Trinity Church at the end of Horns Road. Beforehand we dressed in our best clothes. (My mother had a new outfit and a hat which looked like a pom-pom dahlia). She produced buttonholes for us and my father took our photographs. Then presumably we had to walk up Tuffley Lane to the Fox and Elm and travel in our finery over to Stroud on the bus. I had never attended a wedding before, so was enthralled by the service. Perhaps the strangest aspect in retrospect was to see Aunty Mue just watching from the other side of the church railings as the bridal party came out of the church. Neither she nor Lewis came into the church or attended any of the celebrations later in the day on the basis that they had no suitable clothes to wear and didn't want to show anybody up.

There was a reception at a Cotswold pub somewhere in the Amberley and Minchinhampton area, and a buffet was served. The star of the show was Aunty Gert who, unlike her sister, was not above dressing up for an appropriate occasion, and came swathed in blue and wearing a hat my mother said made her look like the Sheikh of Araby. She was very taken with the buffet, and in particular what she called, and kept recommending as "sparrowgrass sandwiches". She did the rounds and made sure she had spoken to everyone. For some reason that day she had been impressed with someone she had met through her own church and kept repeating this person's bons mots in every conversation: "Mrs General Jones d' say.....Mrs General Jones d' say..." seemed to reverberate around the assembly.

I think it must have been later that very day that we went up with my grandmother to visit and get to know Marion's parents. We were shown the house which Maurice and Marion were having built on a plot of land her parents owned at the bottom of their large garden. It was complete with a dark room and car inspection pit!

The other big family event that Summer had been our holiday at Whitsun – this time a return to Littlesea Holiday Camp near Weymouth, where we had stayed in 1960. Our caravan was smaller and less well positioned than on our previous visit, but there were advantages to the camp which had escaped me before. In the first place, it had a small cinema, and one rainy night we watched a World War 2 submarine film. There was also a book section to the camp shop, which I took to browsing. My interest in fact alighted on a novel called "The Heart of Jade" which, from the cover, was set under the empire of the Aztecs. There were other aspects of the cover which implied to my mother that it was not a book suitable for an 11-year-old, but, despite her urgings not to waste my pocket money, I went ahead and bought the book, convinced that it would enhance my understanding of Latin American history. It was immediately confiscated by my mother, who said she would keep it "until I was older!" She refunded the purchase price.

Most other associations with the holiday are by way of pop music. "Juliet" by the Four Pennies, "You're My World" by Cilla Black, "Walk on By" by Dionne Warwick and (best of all, as far as I was concerned) "Move Over Darlin'" by Doris Day were all high in the charts. It was whilst we were at Littlesea that (having referred to their rival recordings of "Anyone Who Had a Heart") "The Daily Mail" reported on its front page Dionne Warwick's considered opinion: "Cilla? She ain't got the voice!"

One evening we went for a walk along Weymouth Pier (a much drabber and more functional pier than either of the ones at Weston) and there we espied a juke box. Egged on by my mother and sister, I selected the Beatles' "Can't Buy Me Love", not realising quite how amplified the sound would be when the stylus engaged with the vinyl 45. It boomed out over the harbour, and, whilst this was a delight to myself and my co-conspirators, my father stalked off, too embarrassed to be associated either with us or the record. By the high Summer, however, even he had mellowed to the extent that when "A Hard Day's Night" came to the Odeon, not only did I go to see it with Gerry Connor and Jimmy Bonfield, but my mother and father took Ros and I to see it again a few days later – and we sat through two full showings.

Though I did not know it at the time, a shadow hung over our family for much of 1964 – quite separate from the loss of Uncle Joe and difficult to place in the positive context of Maurice's wedding, the success of my year at Lower Tuffley Junior School, and the general air of optimism engendered by the Beatles. My mother was ill. On arriving in Gloucester, we had registered with a local doctor recommended by the Powickes: Dr Norbert Glas, who was Austrian, probably a refugee from Nazism, and was a herbalist and anthroposophist, quite hostile to trends in modern medicine. I had little to do with him during our first year in Gloucester, but my mother seemed to make frequent visits up Tuffley Lane to his surgery. It was only after I had moved on to my grammar school that one day my mother explained that she was "very ill" and would in fact be having an operation. (This was for a hysterectomy – undiagnosed by Dr Glas for many months, whilst he tried first one alternative remedy and then another to treat whatever symptoms my mother had complained of.) The story of that crisis in our lives is for another time, but it is always a shock to me when I think how unobservant I must have been regarding my mother's health and mood, and how very good my parents must have been at shielding us from worrying news.

CHAPTER 27

Amongst the challenges of my year at Lower Tuffley Junior School - the stresses of being so far behind and then preparing for the 11 plus, the entirely new social life into which I was thrust, and the emergence of amateur drama as a major feature in my life – there were darker and more sobering experiences. There had of course been Uncle Joe's death. In November came the assassination of President Kennedy.

Despite my support for "the grocer's son" as opposed to "the millionaire's son" back in 1960, by 1963 I, together with most of the world (outside the USA at least), had fallen under the spell of Camelot. "Ich bin ein Berliner" passed me by, but his preceding visit to Britain made a big impression. One Saturday I had been fascinated to watch the tv coverage of Kennedy's arrival at Prestwick after calling off in Ireland. He was met by Mr Macmillan, and there was much talk of special relationships and the close ties between the two politicians. The media had also heightened our feelings of involvement with the Kennedy family earlier that Summer with its reports on the loss of their third child.

It was only a couple of months later, on a Friday evening, when I was actually in the toilet, that I heard my mother almost screaming up the stairs: "Jack, Jack, they've shot Kennedy!"

A very few minutes later, as we all sat stunned in front of our tv and Richard Baker described what was understood to have happened, the newsreader received a telephone call on screen. He listened, put down the receiver and said: "We regret to announce that President Kennedy is dead".

It felt like the most awful world event that I had experienced, though in the tv age I had been aware of wars, famines, and revolutions for years before. It was the personal nature of the catastrophe which made it so shocking, and when, on the Sunday evening, the News carried footage of the shooting of Lee Harvey Oswald, as it later emerged by Jack Ruby, we seemed to have descended into a nether world of horror. There was also a sense of panic in the air for at least a few days, as stories of Oswald's Russian connections emerged and once more rumours of World War 3 began to stir. The "they" of my mother's instant reaction to the news of the shooting were a continual presence throughout my childhood. Whatever went wrong in the world, the undifferentiated "they" were responsible, and "they" were not just the Russians, who were but one aspect of the dark forces who threatened us. "They" had shot Kennedy even before the Russians came under suspicion.

At school on the following Monday Mr Alderton of course referred to the events over the weekend and we had special prayers. Everyone seemed deeply affected. For the State Funeral we were given the day off and again I followed the tv coverage from start to finish, absorbing every drum beat and every angled view of the slowly gliding gun carriage, and of Jacqueline and the two surviving children.

Forever, if inappropriately, linked to the story of the Kennedy assassination were two completely unrelated events the following day: the first ever episode of "Dr Who" and the first performance on "Thank Your Lucky Stars" of "24 Hours from Tulsa" by Gene Pitney. The darkness of both seemed to chime with prevailing atmosphere, though "Dr Who" later lightened its tone and became a regular feature of our Saturday afternoons, along with "Grandstand", "Juke Box Jury", and "The Billy Cotton Band Show", as well as an inter-generational cult second only to the Beatles.

At the end of February a more domestic tragedy struck, again causing Mr Alderton to conduct a special and very solemn form of school assembly – this time with our singing of the verse of "Oh God, Our Help in Ages Past" which was normally omitted:

"Time like an ever-rolling stream,
Bears all its sons away;
They fly forgotten, as a dream
Dies at the opening day."

A very few minutes before I had been greeted as I entered the school playground by Gerry Connor and Tim Parrott, the former uttering the words: "Hey. Have you heard the latest? Billy Mitchell is dead!"

Billy Mitchell was one of the boys in the form with whom I'd had least to do since I joined the school. In fact, for some reason he had taken a dislike to me, stating that he did not like white as a colour, and didn't care much for the kid either! However, only very recently he had at least been polite, and I'd hoped that whatever offence I had given at the outset had been forgotten. He was a pleasant looking child, who had a round face and a little puppy fat. In my mind's eye he is always wearing a faun jumper with a shawl collar. Apart from his attitude to me, he seemed to get on well with everyone else and, whilst not near the top of the class, seemed to work hard. His parents had recently moved house from Podsmead nearer to the city centre, and this necessitated a bus or cycle ride for Billy to and from home.

The evening before (a Monday), making that journey by bike, he had collided with a bus, and, according to the rumours which seemed to come out of nowhere, had been crushed. At the top of the front page of "The Citizen" on the Tuesday evening there was a short account of the accident in dark type which recorded that on arrival at hospital "William was found to be dead", though, as Tim pointed out, Billy had never been known as William.

The reaction of the class was shock, rather than grief. Maybe eleven-year-olds would grieve only over the death of a member of their own family. Somehow, we soldiered on towards the 11 plus which was then only a matter of weeks away. We were told by Mr Bolton that none of us was to attend Billy's funeral, which took place the following Saturday, and my mother told me, as I went to bed that first day after the accident, to try not to dwell on what had happened.

When Saturday came, I remained all morning in our back room at 18 Epney Road, to avoid seeing the funeral procession (which, nevertheless, Jimmy Bonfield was able to report had included a lot of black cars). Whatever I had done that morning would have seemed inappropriate. In the event, I sat by the fire listening to the wireless, which was broadcasting from the Ideal Homes Exhibition at Earl's Court and featured, in particular, Cilla Black's "Anyone Who Had a Heart".

If anyone in our class suffered, it was almost certainly Mr Bolton. No less an authority than his son (who was several years older than us) was said to have reported that after the funeral his father went home and went to bed in tears. He later agonised over whether a road traffic advertisement, which one of the class had designed, should be placed on the classroom wall – just in case Mrs Mitchell came in to see him (as she had been invited to do). At the end of the school year in his last farewell to us all, he mentioned Billy's death as the one great sadness of the year.

We used to see Billy's younger sister making her way to the infants' school along the pathway running through our school grounds. It was whispered in the playground that she didn't know Billy had died, but she knew he was never coming back.

Within the class I don't remember Billy's death being discussed or dwelled upon after the first week or so, and life seemed to revert to normal very quickly. There was no pall of sadness or depression at the time of my own birthday party less than a month later.

For my own part, I did not feel traumatised by the event, and yet every one of the many years since, on the anniversary of his death, I have spared Billy a thought, and it is something which is always referred to, if Tim and I recall our year together in Mr Bolton's class.

CHAPTER 28

Once the 11 plus was out of the way, it was inevitable that there would
be a relaxation in the intensity of our education, but that is not to say
that we found our time any less taken up with improving activities, or
that the expansion of our horizons proceeded at any less break-neck a
pace. Apart from lessons in standard topics, the continued need to
deliver classroom talks and read the maximum and minimum
thermometer, there was our introduction to French and the production
of our own literary masterpieces. In addition, three educational trips
had been arranged by Mr Bolton – three trips which apparently were
undertaken by his form every year.

The first was to Whitcombe Waterworks, which were located a few
miles to the east of Gloucester and, given the sorry state of our
domestic water supply, was a subject of no mere academic interest. We
processed along the sides of various settling tanks and were told how
sewage was treated. It was no surprise to learn that Gloucestrians had
to drink reprocessed effluent.

Of more interest to me was the second trip, which was a tour of
Gloucester Cathedral, which was conducted by an ancient verger called
Mr Mooney. We explored every part of the cathedral, including the
Norman crypt, the whispering gallery behind the great East Window,
the nave with its pillars marked by medieval masons and scorching
from ancient fires, and the cloisters with their glorious and (in their
time) revolutionary fan vaulting. The West and the East Windows were
explained to us in detail, including the earliest depiction of someone
playing golf, and we also became expert in the functions and
construction of flying buttresses! Within a few weeks I was able to
regurgitate everything we had been told for the benefit of Aunty
Dorothy and Uncle Brian, who were making one of their fleeting visits,
and were delighted to visit the cathedral before taking the bus back to
Epney Road for one of my mum's teas.

It may or may not have been the tea on that occasion, but I managed
once more to embarrass my parents by speaking out of turn. One of
my mother's regular stand-bys for tea, whoever the guests were,
happened to be coconut pyramids, which were always presented

browned from the oven and with a cherry on each top. My father and Stan Skinner had taken to referring to these as "teenagers", in view of their firm upstanding shape. Never having registered what they were referring to, I of course felt justified in repeating this to my uncle and aunt. It is possible that Brian and Dorothy, being rather unworldly, were no more alert to the erotic connotations than I was, or alternatively I may have undermined all the good work I had done with my lecture on medieval architecture!

The main school (or rather, class) journey for the year was to London. If anything epitomised the difference between Church Street and Lower Tuffley Juniors, it was this. After one painful experience of trying to shepherd his charges around the capital, Joner had declared to assembled parents that he would never undertake it again. Admittedly, he and three other teachers would have had to deal on that occasion with a school of perhaps one hundred boys, whereas our journey in July 1964 involved a class of about thirty-five under the joint control of Mr Bolton and Mrs Alderton. It also involved months of meticulous planning by Mr Bolton himself, plus his years of experience in conducting similar trips. The sun shone, and the whole day was an unqualified success.

We pupils had been well prepared for the occasion. We had a booklet of printed pages telling us all about the various items of interest we would be seeing (and for which we each had to design an individual cover, mine showing what I imagined Nelson's Column to be like). We were also instructed on what to look out for on the rail journey to Paddington. This included the Stroudwater Canal, with which I was quite familiar, and concerning which we learned an apposite poem: "The Old Canal" by W.H. Davies, a Welsh poet who had taken up residence in the Stroud Valleys. We also had to learn (and this was far more difficult) Wordsworth's "Composed on Westminster Bridge" to prime us for one of the highlights later in the day.

Once we had arrived at Paddington, Mr Bolton marshalled us straight to the underground from which we emerged a few minutes later at Trafalgar Square. We were then marched down Parliament Street, past Horse Guards Parade and the Cenotaph to Downing Street, down which we plunged (as you could in those days), before making our way (from its far end!) to The Mall and then Buckingham Palace, just in time for the changing of the guard. We then devoured our packed lunches sitting in Green Park. All this time I was taking crazy angled shots of landmarks, using my new camera: a present from my parents for passing the 11 Plus. At my side was Tim Parrott who was my partner for the journey. Unfortunately, on the tube to Trafalgar Square, such had been the excitement of the journey, and such was his proximity to my side, that he vomited, splashing my bare legs in the process. I dried out in the sun, but remained malodorous for the rest of the day.

From Green Park we took the underground to the embankment near the Houses of Parliament, where we boarded a pleasure steamer which took us, with appropriate commentary on everything which we passed, all the way to the Tower of London, where we enjoyed a lengthy tour, taking in Beefeaters, the White Tower, the crown jewels and Traitors' Gate. My memory becomes a little hazy after that, but I'm fairly sure that we returned by tube to Westminster, if only to view Parliament and Big Ben from the outside, before going back to Paddington, where Mr Bolton had arranged to collect packets of sandwiches from a British Rail kiosk for us to eat on the train home. Even in those days British Rail sandwiches had a poor reputation, and they certainly lived down to it! I would not forget the stale thinly cut beef between white sliced bread which curled at the edges.

And so we returned to Gloucester Station, and thence by coach to the school − a tired, but happy group of children, who had achieved everything expected of them that day, but throughout the year too. We were returning to a few more days at junior school, before our lives sundered between four different grammar schools, and even those of us who proceeded together to the Crypt would find that by Christmas, separation into three parallel forms would almost have dissolved the bonds of friendship which we imagined to be so close.

We returned to our last Summer as children, in a country on the cusp of a change from the "Thirteen Wasted Years" of Tory Rule (we had known nothing else) to Harold Wilson's "white heat of technology", yet in the context of the continual excitement at what was the real revolution for us: that burgeoning pop scene. It was a crossroads where old and new mingled, where those who had been the top and most privileged form in a junior school, would soon become the minnows of a much more intimidating institution, where "The House of the Rising Sun" could reach No 1 from nowhere, and yet jostle for supremacy in the charts with the likes of Louis Armstrong's "Hello Dolly". It was a world in which I was attuned to and thriving in a drab 60s suburbia, but with Rodborough and the Stroud Valleys just the other side of the Cotswold escarpment - a mere bus ride away, though by now feeling decades distant.

Printed in Great Britain
by Amazon

51182858R00108